# Papago Woman

ℓ

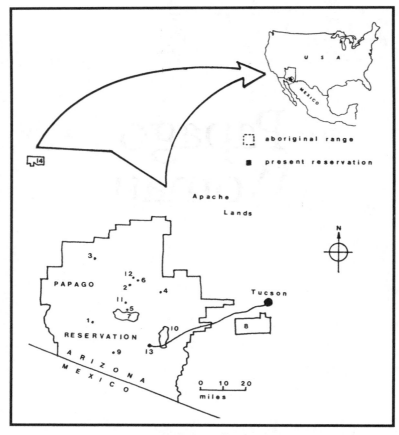

## Map Key and Synonymy

1. Buffalo Head   Pisinimo
2. Burnt Seeds   Santa Rosa
3. Cleared Land   Kaka
4. Hackberry Pond   Comobabi
5. Mesquite Root
6. Narrow Place   Aatci
7. Quijotoa Mountain   Carrying Basket Mountain
8. The Spring   San Xavier Reservation
9. Where the Owls Hoot   Tecolote
10. Where the Rock Stands Up   Baboquiviri Peak
11. Where the Water Whirls Around
12. Where the Willows Grow   Anegam
13. Sells
14. Gila Bend Reservation

*Prepared by David Irving*
*Denver Museum of Natural History*
*Anthropology Department*

# Papago Woman

An Intimate Portrait of American Indian Culture

## Ruth M. Underhill

WAVELAND

PRESS, INC.

Long Grove, Illinois

For information about this book, contact:
   Waveland Press, Inc.
   4180 IL Route 83, Suite 101
   Long Grove, IL 60047-9580
   (847) 634-0081
   info@waveland.com
   www.waveland.com

**Back cover author photo:**
ACC. 90-105 - Science Service, Records, 1920s-1970s,
Smithsonian Institution Archives.

# Foreword

## About the Author

At the urging of the editors of this series, Dr. Underhill has provided a brief biographical statement in a more personal vein than we are usually privileged to include in a case study. We felt it was particularly important to have such a statement with this study for it gives us further insight into her relationships with the Papago at a time when anthropology was just beginning to be recognized as a discipline, and it shows us something of the anthropological context as she experienced it. Much has changed since that time—for the Papago, for the author, and for anthropology. But Ruth Murray Underhill is active, vigorous, still producing anthropology, and can look back upon a long and illustrious career.

She has always been an activist, as her own biographical statement will show. She went directly from college into social work and there developed a need to understand more about human beings and their problems. This led her to the Department of Anthropology at Columbia University, where she studied under Franz Boas and Ruth Benedict, taking her Ph.D. degree in 1937.

Under Columbia auspices, she did fieldwork first with the Papago, the subject of this volume, then the Mohave. Then came years of work with the United States Indian Service, lecturing to the white teachers who had actual contact with the Indian children and writing a series of pamphlets for Indian schools describing the customs and achievements of certain tribes.

A change of administration put an end to this project. Dr. Underhill's final official working years were spent as Professor of Anthropology at the University of Denver.

She has produced a television series on American Indian cultures and is the recipient of an award for promoting intercultural relations. In 1962, she was awarded an honorary LL.D. degree by the University of Denver and in 1965 received the honorary D.Sc. degree from the University of Colorado at Boulder.

After official retirement, her time has been spent in writing. She has published many books and articles, both for the profession and for the public. Her latest (1971) is *So Many Kinds of Navajos.*

# About the Book

*The Autobiography of a Papago Woman* was first published in 1936, as Memoir 46 of the American Anthropological Association. It has since then stood as one of the autobiographical classics in literature on the traditional cultures of native North America. As a now scarce memoir, available only in university libraries and some private collections, it is infrequently read by undergraduate students in introductory anthropology courses or in courses on American Indian cultures. The publication of the autobiography as the core of the present case study makes the material widely available. Fortunately Ruth Underhill has been able to add substantial sections of description and interpretation, as Parts I and III of this case study. These sections will make even more vivid for the student reader what Chona, the Papago woman, says about herself in her autobiography through the ethnographer. She is about ninety years old as she recalls her early life, which probably began around the mid-1840s. Part I sets the stage with a sensitive description of how the ethnographer experienced Papago culture in the years 1931–1933. Though written forty-five years later, these pages bring the situation, the people, and the ethnographer's experience into sharp, vivid focus. Part II is the autobiography itself, unchanged from the way it was first published forty-two years ago. The original introduction to the autobiography is retained as well. Part III extends our understanding of the Papago by drawing our attention to features of Papago life that are touched upon in the autobiography but that benefit from explicit expansion.

Included in this case study is a foreword by Ruth Benedict, written about 1933 but never before published.

GEORGE AND LOUISE SPINDLER

# Foreword to *The Autobiography of a Papago Woman* by Ruth Benedict

The daily task of the ethnologist is with the alien ways of acting, the alien ways of thinking, that are the traditional heritage of different peoples. His business is to set down this heritage as best he can, and no one knows better than he the difficulties of the task. Too often he records only the formal outlines of the strange culture he has encountered, the techniques of planting and of hunting; the form of marriage; the duties of relatives; the ways of doing magic and of getting supernatural power. Too often in this businesslike account everything is told except the essential matter; all that is left out is what manner of men and women these are, and how they live and die and pursue their chosen goals.

Dr. Ruth Underhill, during three years of ethnological work among the Papago, has not been content to make only the formal report of the culture of these desert people of the American Southwest. From the lips of an old woman, her friend and confidante, she has taken down the story of her life. Hardly at any point was this life touched by our white standards of existence. From beginning to end it has run a different current, filled with achievements, with joys and sorrows that arose out of the substance of life among her people. Her story—whether she is telling of being given to a husband she has never seen, or of her father's adopting his enemy's scalp into the household, or of the village ceremonials—sacrifices nothing of the accuracy of an ethnologist's formal account; but it has also what the latter can hardly attain —the breath of life.

Dr. Underhill has put together in an ordered sequence from childhood to old age the countless confidences of this old woman of the Arizona desert. The ethnologist may learn much from this autobiography that in other accounts tantalizingly escapes him; he need not fear a journalistic distortion. The reader who is interested in the things men live by under other codes of right and wrong, other hopes and terrors, will find here a real story, one of the few that has been put in print, of a human life among a primitive people.

RUTH BENEDICT
ca. 1933

# Preface

My life, up to college age, was passed at Ossining-on-Hudson, thirty miles from New York City. Never mind the date. It was before World War I, therefore before the rise of unions, World War II, the TV, and Vietnam. To my mind, even yet, that was a halcyon period. The Civil War was long over. For us in America, the greatest country on earth, the dollar was stable, prices moderate, and hired help plentiful.

Girls wore long skirts down to their ankles. They walked to school and church and some drove about in pony carriages. There were occasional trips to Europe, but not the expensive progress between hotels which many people imagine. If one took a slow steamer and stayed in boarding houses, it cost less from New York than the Grand Canyon. And it did show you other people beside Americans.

My education was at a girls' school and then Vassar College, where I specialized in language and literature. After graduation, the choice was marriage or teaching. Both looked tame. I jumped at the chance to be an agent of the Massachusetts Society for the Prevention of Cruelty to Children, working with Italians. Respectable as this sounds, it took me into tenements, sweat shops, and Children's Court. A real chance to know people!

Adventure called me to New York, where I mingled with more people—"charity cases," Marxian enthusiasts, and psychoanalysts. Then a rest period of wandering and mountain climbing in Italy, Germany, and England. That ended with the bang of World War I.

Against parental opposition, I managed to get an appointment under the civilian Red Cross. I was part of a unit sent to north Italy to care for the orphans of Italian soldiers. No war there, only village tragedies and scarcity of food—except goat cheese, chestnuts, and wine.

I came back to a country where the days of cheap food and service were over. A succession of jobs in social work brought the human problems starkly before my eyes. Some writing and publishing did not help, nor did a brief marriage. My final conclusion was: "I need to know more about PEOPLE."

There stood Columbia University and the fall term was beginning. I tramped through its timeworn halls, from one department to another, with my question: "What subjects do you teach that will help me to understand people's behavior?"

Most answers sounded like a proclamation of ultimate truth. But they were stereotyped—right out of a book. Until I reached Anthropology and the late Ruth Benedict. She was a kind and beautiful woman as well as learned. She said: "Come in here." And that settled it.

Three years at Columbia, under Ruth Benedict and Franz Boas, were full to bursting with discovery and achievement. After the first came the test of persons who had shown determination to go the whole way with anthropology. Each was given some group to investigate. The younger members of the class, mostly males, were soon given their assignments. Dr. Boas had some question, perhaps, about a mature woman who had specialized in languages, but he was one of the early sympathizers with women's ambitions. He asked, "Do you have a car?"

"An old one."

"Well, our funds are low, but there is a small tribe of Indians in Arizona. Perhaps you could drive there."

"Of course." I did not even ask the name of the tribe, but started for the western country so much less known to me than Europe. So I met these hard-working but poetic Papagos and fell permanently in love with them.

I could have spent a life among the Papago, but in those days we did not get grants easily, as students do now. Finally I moved, at Columbia's direction, to the Mohave. Then the Indian Bureau took me in. I spent thirteen years traveling among the reservations studying the tribes, which are all so different with their customs and needs. In the summers, I lectured to the "Anglo" teachers who were anxious to learn all this and had no time. Finally, I wrote a series of pamphlets picturing the various tribes for schools which I hoped would be both Indian and non-Indian.

My teaching career ended with five years as Professor of Anthropology at the University of Denver. When teaching was finally over, I went straight from the Anthropological Conference in Vienna to the plane that would take me on the first leg (they were centipede legs) of a trip around the world—Israel, India, Australia, New Zealand! No country would let me stay more than three months without special permission. Anyway, I wanted a drink of ice water! So back to Denver and down to writing.

The present paper may be one of the last I write. I wish to preface it with the following:

My visits to the Papago took place in 1931–1933. The introduction following, given as Part I of this case study, is written from memory in 1978 and is of a different material from my talks with Chona. Those I took down verbatim from her lips. I translated her words as best I could, with her help and that of companions spieling Papago, Spanish, and English. I have never tampered with them since, nor with the words of ceremonials taken at the same period.

The introduction is different. Here I write from memory some forty-five years later. The scenes and their meaning I shall never forget. But the exact dates and places! I may well misplace some of them and give offense. And the people! I have changed all names except that of Chona. This whole introduction, meant to show her environment, is a memory picture of my own—true in essence.

RUTH M. UNDERHILL

Denver, Colorado
July 1978

# Acknowledgments

This account would not be complete without giving full credit to those who helped in the production of the study.

Dr. Bernard Spilka, Professor of Psychology at the University of Denver, did much to bring Chona to the attention of publishers. Dr. Donald Bahr of the Department of Anthropology, Arizona State University, provided data on the modern Papago school situation, helped with photographs, and assisted with place names for the map. Mrs. Joyce Herold, Curator of Anthropology at the Denver Museum of Natural History, most kindly reproduced some of the photographs taken by the author. David Irving, Denver Museum of Natural History Anthropology Department, made the map and helped to select and process pictures. Above all, I would like to thank Mrs. Mary Coen of Denver for the research, typing, and general filling-in necessary in a publication of this sort.

We wish to thank the National Council on Family Relations, 1219 University Avenue Southeast, Minneapolis, Minnesota 55414, for permission to use material from Dr. Underhill's "Child Training in an Indian Tribe," in *Marriage and Family Living,* Vol. IV, No. 4, 1942.

Thanks is also given University of California Press for permission to quote verses from the author's *Singing for Power;* and to University of Chicago Press for permission to reproduce a verse from the author's *Red Man's Religion,* p. 245. Copyright 1965 by The University of Chicago. All rights reserved.

R.M.U.

# Contents

# PART ONE | Chona: Her Land and Time

I

"I was born there," breathed Chona reverently, "on the Land."

I wish I had some magical, some almost holy translation for the Indian word she used. Land, to me, was a possession to be claimed and fought over by farmers, builders, exploiters—yes—and patriots. For this old Papago woman and her kin, I was to learn, it is the land that possesses the people. Its influence, in time, shapes their bodies, their language, even, a little, their religion.

Our volunteer interpreter spoke softly, "She mean reservation."

He sat smoking on the floor of the one-room dwelling. In fact, we were all on the floor, though Chona and I shared a rough old sheet of the kind the Papago used to weave from their own cotton.

If this had been New York, I would have thought I was seeing dire poverty, for the room appeared to be an unfurnished cellar. But this was Tucson, Arizona, where the most important element of furniture was the sunshine. It glowed on the earthen floor where a few pots and bits of metal could be assembled into a cooking apparatus. It picked out the color in some cotton garments hung on pegs in the windowless wall. It lighted Chona's face, polished bronze between the wrinkles.

Chona was making a basket. She sat on the floor as proper Indian women sit, with legs bent to the side, not spread in the man's style. Before her was a bunch of willow withes and a dishpan of water for soaking them. She was splitting one wand between her teeth, and now she brandished it in a hand as brown and rough-skinned as a tree branch with its twigs.

"Lessa-vation!" snorted Chona. (Her people, I found, used the sound of "l" instead of "r" as do many peoples of the Far East.)

"Lessa-vation! That how Vasindone say. But did Vasindone make our land? No! That was Earthmaker. In the Beginning. He make it for us—Papagos, Desert People! Bean People!"

This tirade had to be translated for me later, but I caught the important words,

*Chona making basket. Photo by author, reproduced with the aid of The Denver Museum of Natural History Anthropology Department.*

"Washington" and "Papagos." I bit down excitement. It was to see this very reservation and these very Papago Indians that my university had sent me to Arizona. Soon I must present credentials and start the dig for facts. First, though, I had hoped for some personal contacts, some thread of friendship to guide me among people whose habits and thoughts must be very different from mine.

One could read about it, of course. Spaniards had moved through the country or past it. Kroeber and Dolores had written about villages near the border. But I had my eye on the stark northern villages with almost no schools or churches. There, Papago was spoken in its ancient dialects. There I might find parts of the past, still alive.

I landed in Tucson, the old Spanish frontier town, now blossoming with modern hotels and stores. My friends there were enthusiastic about the beautiful old church of San Xavier, built by Indians under Spanish direction. It was on the small reservation near Tucson, whose residents spoke Spanish and some English. They often came to town and my friends had frequently had dealings with them, even visited their homes. But the big reservation, out in the desert?

"Well, they're not so advanced. But good, peaceful people. Those who speak some English come in, now and then, to ask for jobs."

(That was in the 1930s, when Indians were not in the public eye as they are today. The reservation lay outside Tucson.)

"What are they like?"

"Oh, big brown people. They speak in soft voices, even the men, and sort of breathe between the words." (How I was to struggle, later on, to attain the technique of Papago breathing!)

Now I had a purpose. "Do you know any of the English-speaking ones?" I asked.

"Well, we employ a yardman, sometimes. And he has relatives. I guess they all hang together." Thus casually did I hear of Papago kinship, the lasting bond, the all-important life-tie of the People.

I met the yardman. From him I burrowed my way from houseworker to errand boy to ditchdigger. Finally, I stumbled upon Chona's kinsman.

His name was Lapai, the Papago version of Rafael. (The People, it seems, shun the sound of "f" as they do "r.") Lapai was just up from Mexico, with smatterings of Spanish and English. His Papago was sufficient for daily needs, and he filled the gap with obscenities so vivid that they seemed almost self-created. His parents had lived through the Indian wars with Mexico—he might have a whole epic in his mind with no words for getting it out. But I could not think of that now.

"Chona," I ventured, "did you really live on the reservation? Did she, Lapai?"

There was consultation, and I was told, "Yeah. 'Till last husban' die."

This statement was the nearest to a sentence that I ever heard from Lapai—or from any of the People. They stepped hesistantly into the morass of the English language with its verb forms and pronouns unknown and unnecessary in the native speech. Many in the remote villages had never heard the sound of English until a few generations ago. Now "Vasindone," which meant the United States government, was seated on the Land and its representatives spoke only English.

There were no schools yet, except those for young children. Adults who had businesses had to learn the language by hearing it. And they did. One or two words would convey meaning enough, as I found when I tried to learn Papago. I came, indeed, to enjoy those quick, short communications filled out by a gesture, a smile, and an aura of good fellowship.

I ventured some of this with my next eager question: "Has she any friends there? Relatives?"

There was more consultation, and Lapai reported, "Have girl. Girl marry, go away. Take kids."

"And no other relatives?"

"Yeah, one son, medicine man. Die."

"Oh, I'm sorry. What was his name?" (I had already become enthralled with the strange, magical names assumed by medicine men. But my question produced a sudden chill of silence. I had not yet learned that Papagos do not mention the names of the dead.)

"Other son, Mexico sometimes."

"Oh, no one on the reservation then?"

Much long discussion between Lapai and Chona. Lapai said, "One man once marry her sister. Sister die. That man marry. Got more kids. He got farm far out. Maybe could go there."

"So! At least she has a brother-in-law."

" 'Brother—'?" Lapai was having trouble. "We don't got that word."

"Not 'brother-in-law'! But what does she call him?"

More consultation. Then Lapai said carefully, " 'Husband-of-my-sister.' "

"Oh!" I gasped.

"But he got name—'Lillat.' Real good name. Don't call dead. Cost bottle whiskey."

This, I found later, was a valuable nickname which could be spoken without calling the dead. The name sounded Asiatic. In later days I worked it down to "Little Hat," i.e., a cloth hat from a clothing store, not the usual cowboy sombrero. The name had cost its present owner a bottle of whiskey.

While I was trying to think of a polite comment, Lapai said, "Got farm. On reservation. Way out."

"Not near government headquarters? That's just where I'd like—" I stopped myself from saying something too forward and tried to think of a courteous way of approaching Lillat. Chona and Lapai went into another consultation. I wondered if I had been too forward, and they would suddenly go silent.

So they did for a minute while I sat and berated myself for failing to learn other people's manners. Then Lapai asked, "You got car?"

"Car? Car?" I was fairly chattering. "Why, yes. You saw it."

Of course they had. Doubtless they could describe every inch of it as they could an animal's trail.

"You know get gas?" said Lapai, the city-dweller.

"Yes, yes. Do you think—?"

Chona spoke some emphatic words, and the translation was: "Not tomorrow. She gotta finish basket and sell. Then go."

My breath of relief could have wafted Chona's cooking utensils across the floor. Apparently they didn't matter, nor did this temporary home. Had Chona and Lapai both been waiting for a chance to get to the reservation? I looked at Chona. She nodded. Evidently the deal was made.

I drove Lapai home and, by slow stages, managed to get more information. The farm of Lillat was an extra property on land newly brought into use. He had a right, also, to land in Santa Rosa, the Burnt Seeds, the old head village.

"Brothers use that place now, but all come back when real year begin."

"Has he many brothers?"

That question was hard to answer, for it seemed that all male cousins of one's own generation were brothers.

"You call them all 'brother,' then? Or 'sister'?" Again my words had stumped Lapai. He finally made me understand that they were called "older" or "younger," depending on whether their parents were older or younger than yours. I sighed at the etiquette I would have to learn if I wished to move in Papago society.

"Is it far?" I asked. "Will there be a place to stay all night?"

Lapai stared. "Village? No. Desert. House."

"Well, I'll take my camping things."

Packing the gear and getting the car serviced, I decided I had better make further preparations. What would be a proper gift to a Papago hostess? Picturing her housekeeping, I decided on a roast of beef. (Beef had a moderate cost in those days.) Potatoes must go with it and then, for a complete diet, a sack of beans.

These were stowed neatly in my car when I drove to Chona's door a few days later. Chona's neighbors, Papago and Mexican, had gathered to load her baggage.

First came the huge cotton sheet, once used for clothing, now for sitting on floor or ground and bedding. Young people, I gathered, held it in scorn; but no old Papago was without it. Next came basketry materials and a walking stick straight from a tree. Then a stoppered jar of water. I had not yet learned never to travel in Arizona without water in the car.

Lapai crawled on top of the load, for it seemed understood that he was going. Chona came last in a cotton dress that looked to me as though it had been washed in cold water a score of times. Assembled neighbors helped her to the seat beside me. Her strong brown feet with their horny nails gripped the floor, and I started the engine. I heard Lapai say softly, "They want go."

It seemed that a whole streetful of women and children were looking at me expectantly. What use to explain that there was no room; the springs would break?

"But," Lapai ventured to object, "when wagons go, *all* go."

"But the springs—"

There was no use in going into automobile construction. I was reduced to smiling head shakes. They did not understand, but they forgave. As I turned the car in a scatter of pebbles and dust, they smiled good-bye. Papagos have learned to smile at the inevitable.

## II

Indian country, in those days, had no paved highways. As we jolted out of Tucson's city limits, Lapai knelt on the pile of baggage while he and Chona pointed out remembered scenes. The old basket-maker had given up her aloofness. With a relative, after months of isolation, words gushed out of her like water from a faucet.

"There! You see?" She pointed to the two hills we were passing, clothed with foliage at the base, bare stones above.

"Black Bottom! That is the name our people gave those hills when we camped here." So Lapai told me, and the name he used did sound rather like Tucson.

"But," he conceded, "your people cannot say it right. How could you? I'itoi did not take you around the country, teaching the names."

At least, that is what he would have said in English. There is no need for the reader to struggle through the obstacle race of my early trilingual conversations. Everything had to be repeated several times, then the English and Spanish words sorted out and supplied with their "f's" and "r's." When I got a word right, the Indians laughed aloud and I learned later that this was a sign of approval, not ridicule.

"Your people lived there?" I asked.

Chona nodded. "Us first. Then Spanish. Then Milgahn."

"And they pushed you out?"

Chona took that without anger. "We moved. To be alone."

My reading had told me that Papagos had never fought with the whites. Perhaps it was the torrid country which kept intruders at a distance. Perhaps it was their own calm acceptance of life which put off fighting until duty really called.

Chona was pointing again. "You see that white spot? On one hill?" I did, indeed, see a white rock.

"That is a skirt, a cotton skirt left by one of our women when she was stolen by the Apache."

"The Apache?"

Chona was still smiling. "Yes. Our enemies. They came every fall, you know, when the corn was ripe, to steal corn and women. Right over that mountain they came, and our men would gather to fight them and rescue the women. Often they could not do it; then our women became prisoners of the Apache."

"How dreadful!"

Chona, however, was nodding peacefully; and Lapai contributed, "Oh, the Apache married them, you know; even if they had wives already."

"And," said Chona, "those Papago women taught those 'Ops' to make baskets like us."

"So that's why one group of Apache makes nice baskets!"

My conclusions about Indian handicraft were interrupted as I clung to the wheel and braced myself for danger. The car had plummeted down some ten feet. The Indians laughed,

"Dip."

"Dip?"

"Hole in the road," Lapai explained. "When rains come, wash road out."

"But can't they bridge it?" That *did* amuse him.

"Maybe Milgahn do it someday. But bridges new. In old times we walked. Don't try to cross in wet time. In dry time, shady. Good for sleep."

At that stage of my acquaintance with the desert, a sandy bed along with ants, horned toads, and goodness knows what else had little appeal. It did, later.

As I looked along this particular dip, I could see that it had once held a good-sized stream rushing down from the hills, oblivious of the man-made road. A few dwarf trees clung to its edges, awaiting revival. Beyond, where the underground water must be low indeed, was a mass of thorny stems curved and tangled like so much old wire. However, they were covered with little green leaves and bunches of something which might have been grapes except that they were only thorny buds. Chona made eating motions.

"Cholla," she told me. "Good to eat in the hungry time. Like now."

"Hungry time now? *June*!"

They pitied my vast ignorance. How could things grow when there is no rain? I thought of my home state, where the fields were already lush with grass or bright with daisies and buttercups. The shoots of corn were already tall. The home gardens had lettuce, radishes, and strawberries. But the Land had never known such possibilities.

When Chona told me her story later, she scarcely mentioned this recurrent scarcity. The Papagos adjusted themselves to it by going to work for the "River People," the Pimas, or by trudging down to Mexico to do labor or sell pottery.

Chona was troubled now as she looked over the landscape. "This is all strange to me. When I was a girl, there were no roads. We girls ran in our bare feet over the Land."

"Running? Where to?"

The land before us showed no trees, no dwellings. The flat gravel glared white under a cerulean sky. Gullies gaped blue with shadow and the few gnarled trees beside them looked like twists of old wire rather than anything organic. The whole scene seemed as brilliant and dead as an exhibition of minerals under glass. Chona shook her head at my blindness.

"Oh, there were places we knew. Where there was some water, yucca, roots, cholla."

I looked. Slowly, as we covered mile after mile, I began to see the Land.

We passed a plantation of greasewood (creosote, *Covillea glutinosa*). I say "plantation" because the bushes, some three feet high, were as evenly spaced as a checkerboard. That, I learned later, was so each one could suck up its share of the water which had seeped far underground. The leaves, half the size of a baby's fingernail, were glazed with varnish to protect them from the sun of the "dry time." Chona eyed them like a relative.

"This is where Coyote came to life. Under a greasewood bush."

"Before the People?"

"Oh, yes. Coyote helped put the world in order. Only he made mistakes." She smiled like a mother.

"Can't you tell me about Coyote? And I'itoi?"

Chona shut her mouth suddenly. Then: "I should not have told you this. These things about the Beginning are holy. They should not be told in the hot time when the snakes are out. The snakes guard our secrets. If we tell what is forbidden, they bite."

This was the beloved Land, the Land that possessed the People and had from "the Beginning"; for their tales tell of no other. It certainly did not coddle its children, I reflected. No rain until midsummer! Food and water to be had only with great labor! Yet it bred people who were strong and tall, used to endurance and able to smile. Later, they were to pass off my tales of Milgahn luxuries, smiling tolerantly. They only half believed them and had no real interest. Their ideas of comfort, happiness, love, duty had been worked out by themselves on a basis of what they knew. They accepted me as an interesting exhibit but scarcely real, because I did not belong to the Land.

We had been driving for hours and lost our way several times. Before us there was only the dusty road going straight toward the blue sky. It was blocked by one of the jagged little cliffs, the "rain catchers," which erupt from the desert now and then. They were, I gathered, discarded remnants of the Rockies whose obese body stretched all the way to Alaska.

"Shouldn't we be getting to the house by this time?' I inquired anxiously.

"Yeah," Lapai agreed, "we passed it."

"Why didn't you tell me?"

"We thought maybe you knew and wouldn't want us to criticize."

I turned the car. After half a mile, there appeared a hillock, then behind it a little adobe house.

### III[1]

The house of Lillat was of adobe bricks. That means lumps of clay dug right out of the Arizona soil, mixed with water and baked in the sun, and laid in rows without mortar. Such buildings have sheltered desert people all over the world, back to the time when the Children of Israel labored on them in Egypt. When I mentioned this to Lapai, he was uninterested.

"She says 'new style,'" he said, indicating Chona. "Her folks built with cactus stems. Round, not square." Chona nodded agreement and I put off my study of ancient dwellings until later.

All this time we were sitting in the car. I had stopped it and was ready to get out, but Chona indicated that we must wait for welcome. And welcomed we were. From inside and outside the house the family appeared. They were in line, the brother-in-law with brown hair and a little mustache in the middle, and to one side of him a big boy and a little one. On the other side, his Spanish wife, willowy in black dress and mantilla, and in a line from her, two girls in the cotton frocks of American schoolchildren.

I had time to see this, for the family stood gently smiling without movement or word. Chona, Lapai, and I got out of the car and stood smiling opposite. This, Chona told me later, was the Papago greeting. One needed to get the feel of the other people to know whether they were happy or sad, what kind of news they brought, whether they had changed since the last meeting. So we stood smiling, absorbing one another's personalities. In fact, there were no words of greeting. Finally, Chona advanced to embrace the woman in black, then the children, then her brother-in-law. Lapai and I were not introduced; we simply received smiles.

Perhaps this was the time to present my gifts. I returned to the car for them while Chona and Lapai were engulfed in the soft babble of conversation. I returned with the roast and presented it to the black-clad wife, Lulita. She took it with a smile and no word of thanks, then disappeared with it inside the house. Next came the beans and potatoes, also taken without a word of thanks. It was only later I learned that Papago has none of the polite phrases which make up the civilization of my people. They see no need for saying, "Excuse me," "Thank you," "So sorry," "Have a good time." One's feelings on these occasions should be plain enough. As for spoken thanks, I learned that this is a cheap way of acknowledging a kindness. Gifts should be repaid with other gifts, not with words. So this family repaid me amply during the months of my stay. Whenever I wished to go and make a special visit or to seek out some person who could give information, I had only to tell one of the family and the answer would be simply: "When?"

This was not the main family farm, I had gathered, but a subsidiary settlement where just a little water from the mountains could be found in summer. So some time must be put in toward cultivating that bit. Inside the house there was no furniture. Already I was beginning to realize how easily people could get by with

[1] Material for this section partially reproduced from Underhill, 1942, with the publisher's permission.

*Papago family and house made of poles smeared with adobe. Photograph by author.*

bare floors on which to sleep and sit. Here, the walls were hung with garments and the essential cotton sheets for sleeping. There were piles of tools in the corners and in the center a depression where stood a granite-ware dishpan filled with coals.

Lillat, the brother-in-law, blew them alight and we all took our seats—he, with the big boy on one side; Chona and I, the two girls, and the small male toddler on the other. The soft interchange of talk began. It seems to me that all Papagos, even the huskiest males, speak in low voices. I remember some western cowboys telling me that the desert spaces demand loud shouts. Apparently the Papagos let the desert speak for itself. They do not need to speak loudly.

We sat while the darkness settled in gently and the flames in the dishpan grew brighter. The heavy door had stood open on the starlit night, but as I looked, a male figure stood there. No one spoke while the host and the visitor recognized each other. Lillat said softly, "There is a place for you."

That was an invitation for the visitor to enter and sit on the male side. He joined quietly in the conversation until I was sure that every step I had so far taken on Papago territory was well understood by all. So were Lapai's steps, and so was everything we wore and used. A few moments later there was another apparition at the door. A new male came in and was seated, then more and more. This was a small village, but the news of visitors and food had gone through it. Every male householder was now present. Finally came the women, all in a group, to sit with Chona and me.

There had been no sign of Lulita. She, I learned later, was at the outside campfire—another sunken dishpan ringed with a fence of thorny cactus. And finally she appeared. She was carrying my whole roast in a pan. Without a word, she placed it on the floor near Lillat; He took out his knife; so did the other men. And as I watched, the roast was cut and everyone had a piece. Plates and forks arrived and seemed to be shared.

I had thought this food might last a week and would serve to pay for my uninvited presence, but such was not the Papago custom. These villagers were all relatives, near or distant; and when one of them had food, they all had food. So the potatoes arrived in another tin pan and then the beans. There was silence while every bit of all this was consumed.

Now it was dark, and through the narrow doorway I could see a brilliant star. And it was cold. I saw people look toward the doorway where a heavy, homemade door hung wide open on the inside of the house. The person nearest it was Lillat's small son of perhaps five years. His neighbor opposite, a young man with the usual soft voice, said to him gently, ' Shut the door."

The child toddled to the door of three rough planks. He gave it a tiny push with no result. I expected his mother, or at least some woman, to rush to the little one's help, but no one moved.

"Shut the door," repeated the young man, who I was to learn was one of the distant kin. "Shut the door. Shut the door."

It took some time, but ultimately with a great whoosh the heavy object fell into place. The toddler turned to us adults with an inquiring look. This was when I would have expected his mother or grandmother to rush to him with endearing praise. "Oh, see what Baby did! My dear, that was wonderful," or whatever those words would have been in Papago. No such thing happened. The little door-pusher, clad only in a brief cotton shirt, stood eyeing his adult superiors and waiting for orders. The only order that came was from his distant kinsman, who had given the first command. He smiled at the child and invited, "Come. Sit down." The place he patted was on the men's side.[2]

I saw plenty of child training during the following years, and none of it was reprimand or scolding. Children were told what to do, and the sheer weight of feeling on the part of the united kin brought forth action. There might be some inconvenience before the child learned, but learn he did.

The food was gone. Smiling, the neighbors rose; and I heard the farewells to which I later became well used.

"I'm going now," said the guest softly smiling. And the host, smiling softly, replied, "Then go." It had all the feeling and kindness of a "God speed you," and meant, "You can go without hindrance." That the guest should come again when there was food was well understood.

That was my first night of sleeping in a Papago house. I had been used to camping in deserts and mountains, so the earthen floor was no hardship. I saw the family arrange itself on one side of the dwelling, father and mother in the middle of the wall, girls on the mother's side beginning with the smallest, boys on the father's.

[2] *Ibid.*, p. 80.

One little old man loitered at the edge of the group. He was called "Salt-in-the-Coffee" and no one ever told me that name without a smile. It seemed that Salt, when he first saw coffee, thought it was stew and salted it. That lack of Milgahn manners haunted him ever after.

That night I did not sleep much. I was part of a group that might have been on the other side of the world—in fact, on another planet—as far as my knowledge of it went. I waited humbly while the family spread their cotton sheets. When they were comfortable, they seemed to go to sleep immediately. After all, they rose before dawn every day of their lives.

Chona and I spread our sheets against the opposite wall. She slept, and I should have been able to. But I lay looking up at the smokehole, a rectangular opening in the roof filled by an indigo sky. In it blazed a star so large in the clear air that it might have been tethered to the house roof. It moved as I watched and others appeared. This, I had already been told, was the Papago clock; and these lights had names unknown to our astronomy.

Now and then I saw Salt-in-the-Coffee pad over to reanimate the coals in the dishpan, his little fawn eyes slanted at me; and I knew that before we left he would have heard from Chona about everything I possessed and did. In fact, the villagers needed such knowledge. I learned about a distant relative who came to live with them and had to be investigated.

"Did you visit the place where he had lived," I asked, "and inquire about him?" I was greeted with a stare.

"No. That would be only talk. We watched him. We listened. That is how you tell how a man is."

Well, I wished that could have been done with some of our national politicians. As for myself, I was now going to be on exhibition, perhaps for the whole length of my stay. Was there any way I could be ingratiating? Better not. In this place, if never before, I was going to be judged by my character as it was.

I heard a stir on the other side of the room. Lillat and his wife had moved together. I saw no more in the dark, and I did not look; but it came to me that all the motions of human life must be well-known to the group. No wondering by children as to how babies came. Of course, they saw the whole process. No concealment of parental squabbles. Not only must the family know of them, but also the village. I began to glimpse the intense oneness of Papago relationships. Everyone knew everyone, down to the last "far cousin." If the group should be broken up and its support lost, how would an individual live?

Perhaps I'itoi had made people to be simple and accepting. I remembered my own youth when, tiptoeing past my parents' door at night, I heard low voices. They were discussing us children, perhaps, our faults and what must be done about them. Or Father's financial situation. That was something about which we were never told. The result with us was a latent hotbed of curiosity and rebellion. Are my people so complex that they cannot afford to share their interests with their children?

## IV

I woke to the sound of gentle chatter and saw the first light of dawn at the smokehole. That first light before sunrise was equivalent to seven o'clock in a city. It meant that one must be up and acting, for by mid-morning the glory of the sun would be almost overpowering. Papagos had learned how to deal with the sun and did not hate or fear it. Those who slept past the dawn light were set down as hopeless drones.

Lillat's family did not sleep late. Before the gray light had changed to pearl, they were up and working. The heavy door was opened and I saw outside the hedge of cactus enclosing Lulita's kitchen. I looked for the pump or stream where we were to wash before eating. I had not yet got the rhythm of Papago life.

There was a rumble outside and I was given to understand that Lillat was going with his wagon for water.

"A government well, two miles away," I was told. "He goes to fill a tank twice a week. This is all new; we never had it until a few years ago."

Chona was scornful: "A horse and wagon to get water! In the old days, we girls ran out every day. Far, far over the Land. For one little pot of water." I thought the youngsters stared at her as children in my home might stare at someone who talked of riding horseback instead of taking a railroad train. But they said nothing. In fact, the family was engaged in house cleaning.

The outdoor kitchen was a circle of branches some four feet high stuck into the earth. They had no leaves at this dry season but thorny scraps had fallen from them, littering the clean sand which was the kitchen floor. One girl swept this floor with a handmade broom. Another straightened the branches and took out broken ones. Their mother, with some tough grass and sand, cleaned the central dishpan which held the cooking fire. Salt-in-the-Coffee came with an armful of firewood picked up from the desert. He laid it at one point which, I supposed, must be the firebox because he went to it so directly.

A pretty picture, I thought. A real primitive, with its few clean lines against gray sand and blue sky. In fact, I had never seen a sky so blue. And cloudless. Had I ever before seen a really cloudless sky? Well, not for a long time. But this blue had been the same since my arrival in Arizona. No rain? But then—?

The wagon was arriving. Lillat backed it up just outside the kitchen hedge. There, in the wagon's rear, stood a huge barrel with a faucet at the bottom. Our host stood proudly beside it, ready to turn the faucet and distribute the government water. Government or not, however, it seemed there was an age-old protocol about water distribution. First the hostess brought a large clay pot with a wide mouth. This was filled from the slowly dripping faucet, then placed in the angle made by branches jutting from the shelter supports. Beside it hung a dipper made of half a gourd with a long handle. I saw later as I sat in that shelter that when a guest arrived, the first thing he did was to dip of the water and drink. This was to show trust and intimacy.

We all drank from the gourd. Then the wide-mouthed cooking pots were filled. Last of all, the hostess brought an enamelware basin to hold under the tap, filled

*Wagon with water tank. Photograph by author.*

it with the sun-warmed water, and handed it to me. I decided to do a hasty wash without soap since I was not sure how soap might be regarded. I finished and was about to throw the water out when hands reached forth to stop me. Water was not to be wasted like that, and each member of the family washed in that same basin before it was emptied.

Then came breakfast. I gathered it was for my benefit, since ordinarily the family would have used these cool hours for work. I had worried about food, having seen the end of the beef. I need not have done so. From a storage pit under the house Lulita produced a roll of dried squash rind. When soaked and boiled, it tasted wonderful. Now it was work time. Our breakfast dishes were rubbed with sand. These remote country dwellers had not yet realized that precious water might be used for mere dishwashing. Lillat and his big boy went to the garden. Lapai left. He was still looking for a job and had found a ride with a neighbor. Chona and I, it seemed, were going to stay. Chona was going to mend some old baskets and mats, and of course I was her appendage.

We women settled ourselves in the ramada. This was a low shed attached to the north side of the house and supported on crooked mesquite poles. Its roof must have been made of other poles. That pile was so thick that no sun's rays could penetrate it, and we could sit as in the coolness of a cave. We sat on our big sheets laid on the clean sand, everyone busy with some activity.

Chona had an old basket to mend. Lulita was cutting up squash rind for the next meal. She showed me how carefully the long soft covering had been peeled from the squash "like you peel a rabbit." (Well, someday I might need to peel a rabbit!) Salt-in-the-Coffee had long been sitting in a corner mending a harness. Salt was a little, stooped man who had once been a hunter but had been injured and given up work long ago. He was a relative of Lillat and had once been the family's oldest honored member. The advent of Chona had subdued him. As time

*Ramada. Photograph by author.*

went on, I came to see that they carried on a rivalry for precedence. They fenced constantly with gentle, soft-spoken words.

This morning Chona was in her element. In me she had the most reverent listener. Even the hostess and her daughters listened with glinting eyes to her reminiscences about old times. Her tones streamed out in a low murmuring voice, and I had three interpreters to help trundle out her ideas. I had hopes of catching some of their talk, for our hostess spoke Spanish and Salt had had his own brand of English for years.

However, more help was coming. Soon the female neighbors came flowing in, each with her "sitting sheet" and some work to do. The one who roused real hope in me was a thirteen-year-old girl. She wore a short cotton dress and sneakers. That last was sign enough of contact with the Milgahn. She was not introduced, but I learned by slow stages that she was one of a large family living at a distance. Her grandmother, however, lived here and Vela (Vera?) had been sent to live with her, "for we must take care of the older people. And in the way they like."

I heard the newcomer speak to Lillat's children and I thought she said, "Hello." I turned to her with a really thrilling hope.

"You've been to school? You speak some English?"

A gentle, whispering voice answered, "Three years. School name Vera. Home name Vela."

"Bless you, Vela. You can interpret—if I get stuck." My kind of English had confused Vela already, but she smiled bravely: "I try."

(I heard after that that Vela was a leader in school. Then, many years later, after I had retired, I heard that she was leading her whole village in public service. I believe it. And I believe also that her service was not performed with drumbeats and banners. From what I saw, she could do all she needed with her gentle voice and smile.)

I ventured to take out a notebook, explaining humbly that we Milgahn wrote so much that we could not remember anything without writing. Thus I got the description of how corn, beans, and squash were stored in a pit for the winter. So it was only lazy people who went really hungry before the rains.

"And the rains don't come 'till midsummer?"

They were amazed that I had not known this, since it was planned by I'itoi in the beginning of the world. In fact, I should have known, for a letter to our National Weather Service gave me the same information. The family forgave my ignorance but I could sometimes catch a tone of kind superiority in their explanations. It reminded me of the tone in my mother's voice when she spoke of a housemaid we had, straight from Ellis Island: "Just an ignorant immigrant, but good-natured and willing." That was in 1900. (In this summer of 1931, the custom of importing housemaids was already in the past.)

I was listening to a group of housewives whose home work was finished before the sun was fully up in the morning.

"Your time is free, now?" I asked enviously. And I thought about telling that someday to a group of amazed suburbanites.

Vela was having trouble translating.

"Free," she stammered. "We always free. But now they must got to make rain."

"Oh! But don't the clouds do that?" I was going to disgrace Chona with my questions, but she put on a brave face. A few more mistakes, and then . . .

Vela translated: "The clouds come because we call them." She stopped me from a question and hurried on, "And we call them with the drinking."

"Dr—?" I got no further.

"Drinking the wine." Here there was a chorus of words I could not catch. "The wine from—" Vela paused to get the word right "—from the Sahuaro, the cactus plant."

"You make wine from it?"

"The old men do. The ones who know. But it is *we* who pick the fruit. We women. And bring down the clouds." I had heard of the famous ceremony but not in just those terms.

"*You* bring down the clouds? You women?"

I have never seen a picture of quiet power more impressive than the one on the lips of six old women under Lillat's ramada.

"Oh, yes," Chona summed up for them. "Men make wine. Men drink. But we get the *bahida* for begin to call down clouds."

## V

I had presented my government credentials. I visited the men in charge of the office and the women who ran the school, all good people—honest and conscientious. They found the Papagos kindly and easy to deal with. They did not know much about their home life because, really, there was no time. All the staff was burdened with duties set down in print and not to be avoided. When they had a month's vacation, how delightful it was to see the wooden house, the elm trees, and the village streets of home. There they could give reports about the Papago march to civilization: "They have a lot to learn, poor things; but they're trying."

One blazing hot day, when I came out of my government quarters, I found Vela waiting. She wore shoes and stockings today and a very clean dress.

"But not school, now," she told me after the smiling silence which was our greeting. "First, rain must come."

"Oh, yes, I hope indeed that rain will come. How do you *stand* this heat?'

I don't think Vela understood that, but she smiled sweetly. "Sun make wine grow. Near ready now."

Then came the message, in soft whispered sentences which I had to extract and analyze. The cactus fruit in the distant groves was ready for picking. Each family would go to its assigned place. With Lillat would be Chona and me— and Vela, too. We would start in two days, all in the wagon. Lillat thought my car could not take the lumpy road. "All right, Vela; I'll be ready."

She must have seen the glorious excitement in my face, but to Vela this was only a regular trip, like Christmas vacation.

We were off soon after dawn. All of us females sat in the body of the wagon cushioned on canvas sheets and sacks of equipment. Lillat and Salt-in-the-Coffee sat in front, occupied in low-voiced men's talk.

The Hungry Moon was almost over. The green things were now gathered under the earth waiting for I'itoi to send the rain. We saw no sign of them as we rumbled on. The unflawed blue of the sky stared down. The bits of mica on the desert sparkled back. The horse had to be pulled up when a turtle wobbled across the road. The girls knew a song about the turtle: "He is very bright, can speak Mexican and Milgahn."

Here, Salt turned with his little triangular eyes shooting sparks. "No sing. Medicine song."

"It's true," Vela admitted. "We didn't learn that at school. At school we learn, 'I love lil' pussy, her coat so warm.' "

"But you don't have cats, do you?"

We were now getting into questions of social behavior which frightened all the children. They took to laughing quietly without words.

We had now reached a series of rocky hollows where the desert had clothed itself in its own kind of verdure. Riots of cholla branches filled a whole hollow, their whips waving aloft with piles of dead branches at their base. The branches rustled and the girls pointed: "Pack rat."

Then came the short, stubby barrel cactus with a field of the little pincushions. Against an incline, the wheel-shaped leaves of the prickly pear seemed to roll along—padded green ovals the size of tennis racquets. Their rubbery plates were covered with bunches of thorns spaced like those on an old-fashioned calico quilt.

"But them sharp," Vela told me. I had already found that Milgahn pronouns were almost too much for a Papago, who never used such things.

Ahead rose the feathery green of a paloverde tree, with a stump of thorny sahuaro cuddled beneath it. Chona and Salt both told me about that in sentences which re- solved themselves into the statement: "Sahuaros have trouble getting started in life. They are so big. Like a fat child, they get sick. But paloverde grows fast like a mother. It bends down the leaves and keeps the wind away."

We had left the dells and the smaller cactus. Before us was a gentle hillside without undergrowth. Its only product was the tall spires of sahuaro, some ten feet high, some twenty, thirty, and then the taller ones with branches like can- delabra. All my family informed me at once: "You see, this is the south side of the hill and the sahuaro grows here, not on the north. That is Coyote's fault."

"Coyote?" Yes, I had heard a bit about that gay roisterer who had so many human failings.

"You see," the tale unfolded, "when I'itoi was furnishing the earth, he thought he would put sahuaro all over. Then everyone could have fruit without too much walking. But Coyote, he doesn't like work." Here, Salt winked at me. Perhaps I was to understand more than the children said. "I'itoi gave him the bag of cactus seeds and told him: 'Go everywhere, place them in order like a park. On south hills, north hills, everywhere.' So Old Man Coyote ran along and he got tired. He was on the south-facing hill. So he dropped the bag of cactus and ran away. Now cactus grows only on the south, never on the north." I nearly said, "With good reason," but Chona broke in sternly, again talking about I'itoi: "It is not winter. The snakes are here." (Oh, dear! I must, I must get back here in winter!)

We passed a north-facing hill, then a south, then we were on a gentle, flat area where the sahuaro grew spaced like pillars for a cathedral. Here was Lillat's camp against a group of rocks where there was shelter from the sun and for a fire. We unloaded the equipment, which consisted of sleeping sheets, dried corn, and baskets large and small. No tent was needed, for the rain was not due until all the fruit had been picked. I saw Lulita eyeing the tops of the cacti where white flowers once had been. Now there were red fruits, pear-shaped, perching against the tops. Looking at them, Lulita said, "Seven days.'

"And the rain comes as soon as the fruit is ready?"

They looked at me with surprise. "Of course." I seemed not yet to have under- stood I'itoi's plans.

It was wonderful to sleep that night under the open sky. Its color was deep indigo, not black; and the stars were almost within reach of one's hand. Around us were camped families of neighbors, each in its own gathering plot held secure over generations. All night, there seemed to be someone singing; for the old men had come, those who knew the songs. I had to understand that though the fruit was sure to ripen and the rain was sure to come, nevertheless the people must sing to help these happenings. So the gentle murmur of songs, forbidden up to now, kept whispering through the still air.

I waked naturally at dawn those days. One does if he chooses to accomplish something before the heat arives. All our women were on their feet, Chona too;

*Cactus pole, as shown me before Papago house (not at Cactus Camp); prickly pear in foreground. Photograph by author.*

and I heard them chattering in the other camps. Lulita, last night, had looked over the cactus poles. These were lengths of wood, each ten or fifteen feet long, tied one above the other into an immense pole. Lillat, who was modern, tied with wire. At the tip, two little slats of wood were fastened—one tipped so as to push the fruit from the plant, one to pull. Each of us women took a pole and a shallow, basin-shaped bucket. The wrens went rustling out of their nests in the cactus holes as we approached, and lizards scampered underfoot.

I had never truly seen the giant cactus, and ants went running over my feet as I stood staring in reverence. The cactus Lulita had assigned to me was some thirty feet high—just mature, I guessed. I went close and saw that it was as thick as the elms on our street at home. But no bark! Its trunk was a thick, rubbery green grooved as regularly as a marble column.

"That's so it can hold water," Chona had made me understand. "When the rains come, it swells. Now, the trunk wrinkles."

But a corrugated trunk was not all. The ridges were punctuated with thorns as strong and white as ivory toothpicks and spaced in clusters from top to bottom. No, I'itoi did not forget the thorns on any cactus. No desert mother has to tell her child not to pick them.

I hoisted my stick and jarred down a fruit—one, two, three. They fell to the ground and splashed open, red skin outside, red jelly inside. The ants were racing to cover that jelly, and I raced to pick up the fruit and get it into my basket,

*Worker carrying cactus syrup, Cactus Camp. Photograph by author.*

*Cooking the cactus syrup, Cactus Camp. Photograph by author.*

meanwhile brushing off the black specks. Salt and the girls and a neighbor woman all stood laughing at me.

"Why, cook all together," Vela explained for them. "Good food."

So I filled my basket bowl with ant-covered fruit, then carried it to where Lulita stood with the master basket. The juice must be cooked lest it spoil. We women made a procession to and fro, plopping our juicy harvest into that basket.

"The sun who walks across that sky every day stops four minutes at the zenith for a rest," so my friends had told me. "However, if the basket is very full, we pickers may stop before that."

And so we did. Lulita had a fire going and a huge pot rested upon it. In went the mass of fruit and ants smelling gloriously in the hot air. We threw ourselves down in the shade of the rocks, almost drunk with heat and satisfaction.

The men, of course, had not been picking. Some had gathered at a little group of rocks and small trees and in low voices were going over the rain songs. I had heard but a few notes of those songs so far. Every time one was started, some older person had stopped the singers. Now, the aged cracked voices went on and on. They called up the white corn, the red corn, and the blue. They caressed the beans and the squash as they ripened. I even heard the sound of the scraping sticks, that rural music made by a smooth, hard stick drawn across a rough, knobby one. It must have been used even before the hollow gourd with its rattling seeds.

Finally, every fruit in the grove had ripened and been picked. Lulita's jar was brimful of juice. And one night, as I lay looking up at the stars, I felt a cold drop on my forehead. Could it be possible? I held my breath. Then Vela called out. From all over the grove came the excited cries: "Rain! Rain!"

It was no more than a few drops, evaporated as they touched our faces. But it was the signal. Before dawn, the wagon was loaded and we were off to the village below the mountain—the mountain which first receives the rain.

## VI

For days the rain came in gusts, its drops seeming to evaporate before they touched the ground. This was the signal for people to move from all outlying farms to the parent village. That of Lillat was the Burnt Seeds, christened by the Spanish colonizers "Santa Rosa." By courtesy, it was Chona's village too, and mine. I had rented a room at the village store. From there, I could see the wagons rumble in, filled with softly laughing people and always with jars of cactus juice to be sent to the council house. There, they would be poured into four tall jars and mixed with an equal amount of water. Four nights they would stand fermenting, watched by old men who knew the proper songs. For the last two nights the whole village would dance, "singing down the rain"; for I'itoi's plans needed this help.

On the night when dancing was to begin, I was at Lillat's house with, it seemed to me, several families. We women were clustered in the kitchen while the men, especially the young ones, were gathered before bits of cracked mirror combing their bushy black hair, arranging silver belts and cowboy hats. I understood enough of the language to hear one ask Lulita, "Do I look well? Will I be chosen?" It seemed that the dance tonight was a ladies' choice. It was said that men in old days perfumed their hands, which they hoped would be grasped.

From the gentle hill where the council house stood, we heard the call of the crier:

Our fire is lit and the sun is gone down.
Our fire is lit and the sun is gone down.
Our fire is lit and the sun is gone down.

> Our fire is lit and the sun is gone down.
> Come together following our ancient custom,
> That the corn may grow, the beans may grow,
> and the squash may grow.

The men in their cowboy boots began to tramp up the hill, but the women remained sitting.

Would we be late? I ventured to inquire; but Chona shook her head. "Men first, then we come, they wait for us. Finally we women march slowly up the incline in a bunch carrying sleeping sheets and babies."

I had seen the council house, which was domed in the old style, called by the Spanish "Half Orange." Now there was a line of poles outside it and a line of fluttering (garments?). No, they were eagle feathers, a sacred possession kept out of sight until this one day. On the flat, smooth space beside the building was the circle of men. There were some fifty or more of them, holding hands and shuffling slowly sidewise. In the center we could see the cigarette of the medicine man beside his tiny fire.

I hung back to watch the women, for each knew just what she would do. Some settled with their babies to watch the night out. The young and even some middle-aged mothers moved toward the circle. They watched the men shuffle past and at the sight of a chosen one—it need not be her husband—each woman stepped in, separated two men and took their hands while the circle moved on without stopping. Chona watched a little sadly. She once had headed the women, she had made me understand, and been the best singer of all. Now a full night of walking and singing was beyond her. Did I want to try it? "No, I will sit with you."

Lillat, however, was a singer—his "medicine" name being "Crooked Lightning." He took his place proudly in the circle and the woman who stepped beside him was not Lulita. Soon the whole circle was punctuated with women stepping majestically to the right while Lillat shook his rattle and the song never stopped.

When I am asked to name some of the happiest moments of my life, I always remember that night under the stars. There was a soft breeze, the precursor of rain. The tiny central fire glowed and the beloved song echoed:

> On the edge of the mountain,
> A cloud hangs.
> And there my heart, my heart, my heart,
> Hangs with it.[1]

Four times, sixteen times, even thirty-two times. No one ever tired of the song that brings rain although there were others to follow it.

Few Indian ceremonies that I know move without pause to a climax. The Papagos stopped to relax stiffened limbs, to attend to babies and other physical needs, including love. From my recumbent position, I saw feet going past me into the bushes, generally two pairs together; for this ceremony brought fertility not only to the crops but to the people.

[1] Underhill, *Red Man's Religion,* University of Chicago Press, p. 245. Copyright 1965 by The University of Chicago Press. All rights reserved.

When the white streak of dawn appeared, the medicine man spoke: "All is well, my kinsmen. Go home, sleep and eat. Tomorrow we dance again."

Few people did sleep that day. The boys were out hunting rabbits. The women unearthed their supply of beans and corn, for when the rains had been thoroughly called everyone would feast. That night we trooped up the hill again. During the dancing, the medicine man came past me and blew some moisture into my face.

"See?" said Chona. "He has the rain."

I thought the drops might be of his own manufacture but was glad to be so honored. And when the white streak of dawn appeared again, the news was wonderful:

"My kinsmen, the wine has fermented," the *makai* said. "Go home. Prepare the feast, for in four days the rain will come."

I asked later about that prophecy and whether it was always fulfilled.

"Oh yes, yes," was the usual answer and old Salt made me understand: "The medicine man, he is wise. Maybe the rain come soon and he says, 'Yes, but I counted from when the wagons arrived,' or it come late and then, 'I meant four days *after* the wine had fermented.' "

At least the faithful were not disappointed that year. There was one later ceremony when the miracle did not occur. I wondered if at last I was to be routed out as a hostile influence. But no, a boy who had been to boarding school had brought back a girl from another tribe, and they were held responsible. There were frenzied days and talk of punishment before the wine really did ferment. I understand that now the ceremony is less formal or at least the fermentation is encouraged with "boughten" liquor.

The sun was blazing when we gathered for the "Sit-and-drink." Here, the men officiated and we women stood in the background. It did not occur to me to resent this, for my companions did not. This climax could not have been reached without their preparations. They were laughing and happy, carrying their babies and with children at their skirts.

Outside the council house the feathers had been removed, and the men were seated in a circle. Not on chairs, of course. The leaders of the four collaborating towns sat cross-legged on the ground, their assistants strung along beside them. Fortunately for me, the Burnt Seeds was the head town this year, receiving its three kin villages. Weeks ago, messengers had visited these towns with sticks to mark the coming days and a long ceremonial speech of invitation. The Smoke-keeper of each town came ready with his acceptance speech. This, like the speeches of welcome, had been carried in memory through generations. They must be recited word for word or the rain would not come.

The important men of the four villages knelt or sat behind the leaders, each in his own sector. In the final row stood the young men, who should have been warriors. They wore cowboy hats and silver belts, and many held a horse by the bridle. I was happy enough to be sitting under the tree which shaded the council house. The women whispered beside me, and the children darted to and fro bringing me news of everything that happened.

We heard the dignified speech of our Smokekeeper, or rather, we did not hear it; for among the Papago sacred words are not spoken to the people but to the spirits. So the beautiful cadence which sounded to me like Hebrew psalms went on softly, was returned, went on again, until each visitor had been welcomed and responded.

Then came the liquor. A way was made through the circle and there entered four young men wearing cowboy hats and carrying willow bowl-baskets filled with the lumpy, red *navait*. I wrote of this once for a New York publication and had my paper scornfully returned: "This author does not know her material! Wine, in baskets!"

Of course it was, in tight-woven willow baskets, which after long use were permanently stained a brownish-red. To each visitor in turn the basket was presented with the invitation: "Drink, Friend. Grow beautifully drunk."[2]

The recipient answered with a song, also traditional. Later, I learned some of these songs which told about the greening of the fields and the ripening of the corn. Often they ended with the singing syllables:

> Therewith were delightful the evenings,
> Delightful the dawns.[3]

The day was almost closing when the four jars in the council house were empty. Men rose from their positions on the ground, some staggering a little. The young men mounted their horses and went tearing through the village. All had been drinking, but there was plenty more wine in the houses. For days, people went from house to house, where the pottery jars and the tin cups were waiting. One was expected to get drunk, Chona told me. He must be livened through and through with the sacred liquor as the earth would be livened with rain. The livening, I saw, caused a good deal of vomiting and Chona pointed: "See? He is throwing up clouds."

I saw no drunken quarreling, though sometimes men rumbled before falling down asleep. They drank and vomited like ancient Romans until all the liquor at the council house and at private homes was gone. So I'itoi had planned it. My women friends shared a jar, and I tasted a little. Like spoiled raspberry jam, I thought privately. It would take a long time and considerable courage to drink enough for intoxication.

I'itoi's orders had been that the wine must all be drunk on this occasion and no more made until the cactus flowered again. It seemed to me that his command was pretty well obeyed. There were three or four days when the men lay about indoors or out, sometimes singing a little, and then sleeping. They and the earth were preparing for real activity.

A week after the Sit-and-drink, the rains came. I believe the medicine man explained that this was four days after *something*, and we all nodded politely. The pet name for this specialist in our district was the "Liar," but it was well not to question him. It was known that he could bring disease as well as take it away.

First came the wind, "bearing the rain on its back." It tore great clouds of dust off the desert, ripping leaves from trees and overturning outdoor kitchens. Then the first drops pounded down like bullets before sky and earth were obscured.

---

[2] Underhill, 1938b, *Singing for Power*, University of California Press, p. 35. Quoted with permission of publisher.

[3] *Ibid.*, pp. 31, 37, 131.

I can best describe it by imagining a wall of solid ice which cut off the landscape, showing nothing but its own watery opacity. Such a wall surrounded our house, but it was liquid. We all huddled inside, even the men busy with repairing tools. The rage of the outpour was over in an hour, and then we saw a film of water over the whole earth. In every gully ran little torrents tossing up spurts of white foam. The roads, I was told, were impassable—the dips raging rivers—and along them flowed old wagon wheels, furniture, tools, anything that had been left out of doors.

The first torrents were over in a week or so. And then came the regular afternoon downpours. They filled the shallow excavations dug to receive water. They kept the children splashing madly and covered with mud all day. They brought out tiny flowers even on the greasewood and flames of yellow on the tall rabbitbrush. In desert hollows that I had never suspected would yield plant life, there were wild oats, wild onions, all sorts of bulging greens which were edible.

The men were wildly hoeing and ditching, making sure that every drop sliding down from the rocky walls should be kept and made to work. At night the older ones, including Lillat, gathered for a while to sing. These were special songs not sung to the rattle, but to the scraping stick. The music seemed to me weird and melancholy, perhaps a sign of its age. It told, in the voices of the green things, how they wished to be cared for, brought out and cherished.

> Tenderly you embrace me.
> I am the red corn.
> In the corner of the field the grass is
> Growing green, growing green.

I went with the women to gather basketry materials. There were slender, tough willow withes which make impenetrable baskets when woven tightly: the black cat claw, too valuable to use except for decoration; the soft but tough leaves of the yucca which makes easy baskets, not having to be pulled through the teeth. All the women were working as steadily as a mill, using the new material while it was pliable. Even I had begun to learn the knot which makes the basis of a Papago willow basket. I had begun to feel thrilled at the sight of a coil which makes a perfect circle and then is stitched to the next.

It was then that Chona started to tell me her life story. That story appears in these pages, brief and concise. It might seem that she spoke briefly and surely from birth through maidenhood, marriage, and old age. Yet the writing of that simple story took three years.

Three years, of course, in short snatches. It meant questioning, suggesting, waiting; for Chona would begin one subject and in the same sentence wander off to another. She had little sense of time, and I had to inquire again and again: "Was this with your first husband? Or the second? Had the railroad come then? Were you at the Burnt Seeds or Where the Water Whirls Around?"

She answered in her own simple words, and I have tried to translate them simply, omitting the flurry of questions and explanation. I learned some Papago as time went on, but I was always helped by friends and neighbors with their Papago, Spanish and at that time, rudimentary English. I feel, nevertheless, that out of all this flurry there came the story as it had appeared in Chona's mind.

# PART TWO | The Autobiography of Chona, a Papago Woman[1]

[1] First published as Memoir No. 46 of The American Anthropological Association, in 1936.

The Papago Indians live on three reservations in the southwest corner of Arizona, near the Mexican border. They belong to the Piman-Sonoran language group and are, in language and descent, identical with the Pima whom they call River People, while they themselves are Desert People. Both were found by the Spaniards in the country they now occupy, which extends from the Gila River in Arizona to the Altar River in Sonora, and which once constituted the ancient Spanish province of Upper Pimeria.

The first important contact of the whites with Pimeria was at the end of the seventeenth century when the famous missionary, explorer, and business executive, Father Kino, established his chain of missions in the Altar Valley. He made a few extensions into the present Arizona, notably at San Xavier, near the present Tucson, and he also toured the whole of Pimeria, not once but many times, distributing cattle and seeds, and baptizing the people with Spanish names. It was in his day that the Papago learned to spend the rainless and hungry winters at the pleasant Altar missions, learning the eighteenth century Spanish methods of farming, which some of them practice to this day.

But the desert country did not attract Spanish colonization. After Kino's time, such Spanish traits as reached the Papago were adopted after their yearly visits to Mexico, rather than forced on them by close contact. Pimeria adhered technically to the Spanish colonial system by which the head man of each village was elected by the people and confirmed in office by the provincial governor. But the lieutenant governor, the sheriff, and the church officers who should have completed the picture were nonexistent. Church services were a form, continued side by side with the ancient ceremonies which persisted with a vitality impossible in the subjugated provinces of Mexico.

This condition of slow acculturation persisted until the Gadsden Purchase in 1853. With this change, Pimeria was cut violently in two, the new international boundary running through its lower portion, the home of the Papago, leaving half of them in the United States and half in Mexico. It was to Mexico that the Papago felt allegiance, for their desert country was still forbidding to both miners

31

and ranchers, and they were left to follow their old customs almost unmolested. Not so with the Pima. Their fertile land, along the Gila, was directly in the track of the gold rush, the trappers, and the Apache fighters. The Pima supplied all these travellers with grain, and early established a relationship which made for swift acculturation not to Mexican standards but to American.

The essential differentiation between Papago and Pima, which is now so obvious, began at this time. The Pima adopted American names and American clothing, and by 1871 had an American school. Meantime the Papago, when they spoke any language at all but their own, spoke Spanish, wore mantillas, and regarded the Altar Valley as their source of culture. More important still, the Pima gave up most of their ancient ceremonies while the Papago continued theirs.

Among the most important had been the ceremonies for war. The marauding Apache, in the hills to the east of Pimeria, had provided constant persecution since Kino's time, but in 1887 they were subdued by the United States, with the help of both Pima and Papago.

After this, scalps were no longer taken, and the important ceremonies of the warpath, of victory, and of warrior's purification were abandoned. But, until the present generation, the Papago continued their intervillage games with the accompanying dances, their cleansing ceremony for food, and their driving away of evil. Even yet, the northern part of the reservation ferments liquor from the giant cactus fruit and drinks it ritually as a magic to saturate the earth with rain. The shamans still practice, and the lay curers dream songs which give each one power over some particular disease sent by a particular animal. Other power can still be obtained, if not from scalps, then at least by the killing of an eagle or the ritual fetching of salt from the Gulf of California. Most of these ceremonies, as they occurred some fifty years ago, are described in the succeeding pages.

The writer made a series of ethnological studies among the Papago under the auspices of Columbia University, covering the periods June to October 1931, February to October 1933, November to January 1934, and October to November 1935, much of the work being financed by the Columbia University Council of the Social Sciences. During most of this time the narrator of the following autobiography, Maria Chona, acted as informant, hostess, guide, and means of introduction to the various villages, in most of which she had relatives or descendants.

Chona is a corruption of the Spanish name Encarnacion, with which the old woman had been baptized on a childhood trip to Mexico. She was the daughter of a prominent leader, José María, nicknamed Con Quien, the name of a Spanish card game. Since the words themselves would have little significance, the nickname has been translated hereafter as "The Gambler." Chona was inordinately proud of this father who had been appointed village chief or "governor" when the Papago first came under American supervision. The Papago custom in most ancient times had been to have a ceremonial leader who performed a few executive functions, but the Spaniards instituted the office of governor and the Americans continued it. Chona's father was the governor of Mesquite Root (*kuitatk*), an ancient village now abandoned, and Chona spent her girlhood there under conditions differing very little from those of pre-Spanish days.

The story of her past was her constant preoccupation, and snatches of it were narrated at every opportunity. Most of it was taken through an interpreter, for, though the writer spoke a little Papago and Chona a little Spanish, it seemed desirable that her words should be transcribed exactly. They were not taken in text but in as accurate a translation as the writer, engaged in a study of Papago grammar, could work out. The wording, therefore, expresses Chona's thought as accurately as may be.

The arrangement, however, is the writer's. Chona is ninety years old and her memory works with the fitfulness of age, presenting incidents in repetitious confusion. The only possible system was to write each one separately, add to it all the amendments which occurred to her during the years of our acquaintance, and then to question her patiently about the chronology until the correct order was worked out. She repeated each episode so often, however, that there was finally no question as to their sequence.

But the matter of accuracy in both chronology and wording being settled, there still remain, in presenting an Indian autobiography, important questions of technique. Indian narrative style involves a repetition and a dwelling on unimportant details which confuse the white reader and make it hard for him to follow the story. Motives are never explained and the writer has found even Indians at a loss to interpret them in the older myths. Emotional states are summed up in such colorless phrases as "I liked it," "I did not like it." For one not deeply immersed in the culture, the real significance escapes.

The writer felt most deeply the objections to distorting Chona's narrative. Yet if it had been written down exactly as she herself emitted it, there would have been immense emphasis on matters strange to her but commonplace to whites and complete omission of some of the most interesting phases in her development. Therefore a pattern was followed. While the essentials of the narratives were retained, it is hoped, at every point many of the repetitions were excised, and the reader is warned of this fact just as he is warned, in the preface to a grammar, that certain phonetic changes regularly take place.

On the other hand, Chona was not allowed to pass over the crises of her life with a mere word. While she had no objection to expressing her emotional states, she took them for granted. But, on being asked, she would amplify in such vivid phrases as "Fear went through me like a snake." Therefore she was frequently asked, and as a result the story has elaboration and emphasis at some points where she would not have placed them, and it stops short where she would have found repetition comfortable. It is an Indian story told to satisfy whites rather than Indians.

There were reasons other than intimacy and opportunity for choosing Chona as the narrator. She is not the aberrant type which so frequently attracts the attention of the white investigator. She accepted her culture completely, and one reason for choosing her was that she had come into contact with so many of its important phases. As a woman, she could take no active part in the ceremonial life. But her father was a governor and a warrior; her brother and one husband were shamans; her second husband was a song leader and composer. And a Papago woman's history is interesting in itself, because, in this culture, there persists strongly the fear of woman's impurity with all its consequent social adjustments.

Chona accepted her status without stress or rancor. She was, however, not the ideal Papago female type, for she was inclined to be independent and executive. In her old age, when such qualities were not taboo, she ruled her whole connection with a competent hand. In childhood she had a minor maladjustment, soon overcome: she started to make songs. Making songs is the Papago achievement *par excellence*, all outward acts being considered merely as a preparation for it. Chona was no poet by nature; she was, in fact, an executive. But she had some urge to accomplish, as the men accomplished, and the proper avenue was song making. So Chona made songs and saw visions, and had to have her shaman's crystals cut out by a minor operation.

She submitted, and found compensation in her life of child bearing and hard work. But in old age the urge came on her again, and again there was no outlet but visions. These later visions are pathetic in their lack of originality, and the songs which she assured me she had composed herself were often changed, only by a word or two, from songs which had been well known for years. Many Papago compose in this way, since song making is a *sine qua non* for success in life. None consider it plagiarism, for song making is the spiritual crown conferred on one who has already achieved in the physical world.

Chona, in her way, achieved. She learned a manipulation of sick babies which was much respected. Very possibly she had observed its performance by her first husband who was a shaman, but the Papago pattern did not allow her to recognize this: she had to dream it, and she did. She picked up other bits of practical medicine, and she had a dynamic personality which drew patients to her. In the end she did all that her culture would allow her toward satisfying her desires and she was not unhappy.

In love, she again showed independence. For a shaman to have more than one wife was standard custom but Chona resented her co-wife. She felt "unnaturally" and against all precedent the same emotions that a white woman is expected to feel "naturally" in such a circumstance. The result was a minor rebellion, soon settled. Chona's life, on the whole, presents a fair picture of the crises which come to a Papago woman, heightened by a dynamic personality.


# I


We lived at Mesquite Root and my father was chief there. That was a good place, high up among the hills, but flat, with a little wash where you could plant corn. Prickly pear grew there so thick that in summer, when you picked the fruit, it was only four steps from one bush to the next. And cholla cactus grew and there were ironwood trees. Good nuts they have! There were birds flying around, doves, and woodpeckers, and a big rabbit sometimes in the early morning, and quails running across the flat land. Right above us was Quijotoa Mountain, the one where the cloud stands up high and white when we sing for rain.

We lived in a grass house and our relatives, all around us on the smooth flat land, had houses that were the same. Round our houses were, with no smoke hole

*Papago woman repairing a basket in front of her dwelling, a traditional brush hut, in San Xavier del Bac, Arizona, ca. 1894. Photograph by William Dinwiddie, Bureau of American Ethnology. Photograph prepared by D. Lindsay, Arizona State Museum, University of Arizona.*

and just a little door where you crawled in on hands and knees. That was good. The smoke could go out anywhere through the thatch and the air could come in. All our family slept on cactus fiber mats against the wall, pushed tight against it so centipedes and scorpions could not crawl in. There was a mat for each two children, but no, nothing over us. When we were cold, we put wood on the fire.

Early in the morning, in the month of Pleasant Cold, when we had all slept in the house to keep warm, we would wake in the dark to hear my father speaking.

"Open your ears, for I am telling you a good thing. Wake up and listen. Open your ears. Let my words enter them." He spoke in a low voice, so quiet in the dark. Always our fathers spoke to us like that, so low that you thought you were dreaming.

"Wake up and listen. You boys, you should go out and run. So you will be swift in time of war. You girls, you should grind the corn. So you will feed the men and they will fight the enemy. You should practice running. So, in time of war, you may save your lives."

For a long time my father talked to us like that, for he began when it was black dark. I went to sleep, and then he pinched my ear. "Wake up! Do not be idle!"

Then we got up. It was the time we call morning-stands-up, when it is dark but there are white lines in the east. Those are the white hairs of Elder Brother who made us. He put them there so we can know when day is coming and we can go out to look for food.

We crawled out the little door. I remember that door so well. I always crawled out of doors till long after I was a married woman and we stopped being afraid of enemies. Then we made houses with white men's doors. But this one was little and when we came out we could see the houses of my relatives nearby among the cactus, and the girls coming out of them, too, to get water.

Those girls had nothing on above the waist. We did not wear clothes then. They had strips of hand woven cloth in front and behind, tied around their waists with a string, for we did not know how to sew them together. Only deer skins the men knew how to sew, but our people had traded this cloth from Mexico and we thought we were very fine. And with good red paint above the waist, it *was* fine. And warm too. But the girls did not put on their paint in the early cold morning. Then they had to work.

There was no water at Mesquite Root; no water at all except what fell from the clouds, and I am telling about the month of Pleasant Cold when the rains were long over. Then our pond had dried up. If we wanted to stay in our houses, the girls had to run for water far, far up the hills and across the flat land to a place called Where the Water Whirls Around. That was a low flat place, a good place for corn, and the water ran down to it from all the hills. A big water hole was there full of red mud. Oh yes, our water was always red. It made the corn gruel red. I liked that earth taste in my food. Yes, I liked it.

The girls used to crawl laughing out of the houses, with their long black hair hanging to their waists, and they would pick up their carrying nets. Fine nets we used to have in those days, all dyed with red and blue. Shaped like a cone they were, with tall red sticks to keep them in shape. When the net was on a girl's back those red sticks would stand up on either side of her face. We used to think a pretty young girl looked best that way. That was how the men liked to see her.

I was too little to have a net then, or even clothes. But I used to help my cousins put the jars in their nets and to put little sticks beween them so they would not break. The boys would stand laughing around and if there was one who was not a relative the girls would joke with him. They would throw gravel at him and run away, and once a girl said to one of my cousins: "Give me that male thing you have and I will put it between my water jars instead of a stick." So we called that man Between-the-Jars. Yes, that is how we joked in the old days.

Then the girls put the nets on their backs and if one was married and had a baby, she put that on top in its cradle board. Some men went with them with their war arrows because there were Apaches in the land then. They all went running, running. If they saw dust in the distance that they thought was Apaches, they went dodging behind the giant cactus. You see, women had to run in those days. That was what saved their lives. Many hours they had to run, and when they came back every family had two little jars of water to last for the day. But we did not mind. We knew how to use water. We have a word that means thirst-enduring and that is what we were taught to be. Why, our men, when they went off hunting, never drank at all. They thought it was womanish to carry water with them.

My brothers went running off, too. Ah, how we could run, we Desert People; all the morning until the sun was high, without once stopping! My brothers took their bows and arrows and went far off over the flat land.

"Run," my father said to them. "Run until you are exhausted. So you will be a strong man. If you fall down tired, far out in the waste land, perhaps a vision will come to you. Perhaps a hawk will visit you and teach you to be swift. Perhaps you will get a piece of the rainbow to carry on your shoulder so that no one can get near to you, any more than to the rainbow itself. Or maybe Coyote himself will sing you a song that has magic in it."

So they went off in their breechclouts and bare feet, running in the dark when they could hardly see the cactus joints on the ground and the horned toads—rattlesnakes there were not in that cool weather. One of my brothers did really have visions. The other used to come back without him, bringing jackrabbits for our dinner. The little boy would come in much later and never tell where he had been. But we found out long, long after, when he became a medicine man, that he had been lying dead out on the desert all those hours and that Coyote had come and talked to him.

When they were gone my mother would come crawling out. She went to the little enclosure beside our house, made of greasewood bushes piled up in a circle and she got the pot of gruel. We always kept gruel in our house. It was in a big clay pot that my mother had made. She ground up seeds into flour. Not wheat flour—we had no wheat. But all the wild seeds, the good pigweed and the wild grasses. And corn, too! Some summers we could grow corn. All those things my mother kept in beautiful jars in our storehouse. Every day she ground some more and added fresh flour to the gruel and some boiling water. That pot stood always ready so that whoever came in from running could have some. Oh, good that gruel was! I have never tasted anything like it. Wheat flour makes me sick! I think it has no strength. But when I am weak, when I am tired, my grandchildren make me gruel out of the wild seeds. That is *food*.

I used to help my mother. When I was very little I began to grind the seeds, just for a short time. When I was ten years old I did it all, for then a daughter should be able to take over the work and let her mother sit down to baskets. But I am telling you about the early days when I could only grind a little. Then we pulled the grinding slab inside the house by the fire and my mother knelt behind it. I picked the dirt out of the seeds and handed them to her, and the pot boiled on the hearth on the three stones that we kept there.

My father was very busy, for he was the chief of our village. People used to bring their quarrels to him, and I remember him sitting cross-legged under the arbor we had to keep off the sun, listening with his head bent and his arms folded, while people talked.

"My daughter disappeared with a man on the last night of the maidens' dance. I want her beaten." "How many stripes?" "Twenty." "Fifteen," said my father. He was a gay man who liked to war and to gamble. He did not like to beat women.

Some days nobody would come, and then he would gamble with the other men,

*Basketry materials. Photograph by author, reproduced with the aid of The Denver Museum of Natural History Anthropology Department.*

throwing the sticks that we use for dice, and then moving stones around a circle as many moves as there were marks on the stick. We used to hear the men singing in a low tone, before they threw, to give them luck.

> Down I shall throw
> The smooth stone I shall move
> Move it to the corner.

They smoked, too, and I can smell their tobacco yet, the strong wild tobacco that we do not have any more. It was tied in a long corn husk, so white, so nice, and when one man passed it to another he said, "Friend!" And the other said, "Friend."

When the sun was high, high, my brothers and my sister came home, and as each one came my mother gave them food. She dipped the gruel out of the pot into a bowl, for my mother was a good potter. We all had bowls in our house. Only my father and my mother ate out of the same one, laughing together, because they liked each other. When my mother dipped out our food she said, "Do not eat it hot. You will have wrinkles." She set mine on the grinding slab to cool. "It will make you industrious," my mother said. My father said to the boys, "Do not eat it hot, no matter how hungry you are. Wait till it has scum on it. So you will be a runner and not a fat man."

When we had finished we did not wash the dishes. How could we, with no water! We scooped food out with our knuckles. The boys used two knuckles because men have time to eat. We girls used three because women must hurry and work. When we were through it was only my father who could wipe his fingers between his toes. That was because he was a warrior and had killed enemies. The rest of us wiped them on the ground and rubbed our hands together. I do not like water on my dishes even now. They feel so smooth.

Then we made our toilet. We washed our faces in a little cold water, but we did not bathe. Rubbing yourself with earth does just as well. Then the older girls painted themselves with beautiful red paint, all in dots and splashes. I went out to play.

I played with the boys and girls who were children of my uncles. Brothers and sisters, we call them. We had no clothes, any of us, but we were not cold. We went to a sunny place and made ourselves dolls of mesquite leaves tied with strings of corn husk for arms and legs and head. We had a little stone for the grinding slab and some sand for the corn. The boys had men dolls and they would take them away and say, "We go hunting." "Well, go," said the wives. Then the boys would hunt all around the village and find a deer bone. "Here is a deer for you."

Sometimes the boys went to get rats. They poked them out of the holes and hit them with sticks. Then we roasted them on sticks with the skins on. Good food, that used to be!

Sometimes we went to run races. We had a good racetrack in our village. Our men had cleared a road that ran across the flat land as far as you could see, and every day they swept it with greasewood branches to keep off the thorns. They had a song:

> The hawk made the racetrack
> And on it we won
> A-a-ah!
>
> We ran with the hawk
> And won a Hawk's heart
> A-a-ah!

All our young men and girls practiced on that racetrack so they could run fast against the other villages. We children ran, too. Every day I ran until I was ten years old and had to be doing the house work.

But we did not stay at Mesquite Root all the time. We were hungry people, we and my father's brothers and his cousins who lived around us. In those winter days my father went to hunt deer and sometimes we all went with him down over the Mexican border to pick the century plant and roast it or to get stalks for our basketry or clay for our pots.

All the year round we were watching where the wild things grew so we could pick them. Elder Brother planted those things for us. He told us where they are and how to cook them. You would not know if it had not been Given. You would not know you could eat cactus stems and shake the seeds out of the weeds. Elder Brother did not tell the whites that. To them he gave peaches and grapes and wheat, but to us he gave the wild seeds and the cactus. Those are the good foods.

There was a kind of cactus called cholla, and when its buds were green we all went and stayed for many days picking them, up in the hills. We pulled the tops of some paloverde trees together and piled greasewood bushes over them to make a shelter and there we lived. My uncles made shelters, too, and my mother and my uncles' wives all went together to pick the cactus. They broke off the new stems with tongs and rolled them around on the ground to get the thorns off, and then baked them all night in a big pit. They smelled fresh and fine when they came out. When the big pit was roasting slowly in the night, the women threw green cholla stems on the campfire ashes to cook. We pulled them out, knocked off the thorns, and ate them hot. Ah, good, good food! We ate nothing else for those three weeks. Green things!

At last the giant cactus grew ripe on all the hills. It made us laugh to see the fruit on top of all the stalks, so many, and the men would point to it and say: "See the liquor growing." We went to pick it, to the same place where we always camped, and every day my mother and all the women went out with baskets. They knocked the fruit down with cactus poles. It fell on the ground and all the red pulp came out. Then I picked it up, and dug it out of the shell with my fingers, and put it in my mother's basket. She told me always to throw down the skins with the red inside uppermost, because that would bring the rain.

It was good at Cactus Camp. When my father lay down to sleep at night he would sing songs about the cactus liquor. And we could hear songs in my uncle's camp across the hill. Everybody sang. We felt as if a beautiful thing was coming. Because the rain was coming and the dancing and the songs.

> Where on Quijotoa Mountain a cloud stands
> There my heart stands with it.
> Where the mountain trembles with the thunder
> My heart trembles with it.

That was what they sang. When I sing that song yet it makes me dance.

Then the little rains began to come. We had jugs of the juice that my mother had boiled, and all the women carried them in their nets as we came running down the mountain back to our village. Much, much liquor we made, and we drank it to pull down the clouds, for that is what we call it. I was too little to drink. They put me on the house top with my older sister. Our jars of liquor were up there, too. The house top was the only safe place.

We heard the people singing over by the council house:

> There sits the magician of the east
> Holding the rain by the hand
> The wind holding by the hand
> He sits.

Then they began to drink. Making themselves beautifully drunk, for that is how our words have it. People must all make themselves drunk like plants in the rain and they must sing for happiness. We heard them singing all day all over the village. Then my father and mother came and stood by the house where we were on the roof, with many relatives. Oh, they were very happy. "Reach us down a new jar from the roof," they said. So my sister handed it down. Then they gave it to drink to all the relatives whom they loved. And each, when he had drunk, sang a song.

The next day a relative came and said: "Your father and mother are out by the arroyo sleeping. Let a child go and stay with them until they wake." So my sister went. My brothers were drunk, too, but we did not know where. At last my father and mother awoke and came home very happy. For many days they sang.

## II

My father told my mother, "There is going to be a big war party. We have sent men to run to the Place of the Burnt Seeds and the Buffalo Head and Where the Willows Grow and Where the Owls Hoot and to Hackberry Pond. They are to meet us in ten days at the foot of the hills where the Apaches live."

My mother was frightened. It was near her time to menstruate and she was afraid it would not be over before my father wanted to go. Then he would have to stay home, because a menstruating wife would weaken him so he would be killed. My mother was careful about that. She went out of the house as soon as it began; she never waited a minute. She never touched my father's arrows nor even looked at them when she could hurt them. So she told him. Then she went straight out to the Little House so it would be safe for my father to mend his arrows and twist a new bow string. I took her food to her, and every day I would ask, "Has it come?" And on the second day she said, "Yes." So it passed and my father could go.

The men went early in the morning before light, and they were gone eight days. All that time we girls and women kept very quiet. When the older girls came home with a load of wood, they never threw it down hard; they placed it softly. We did not laugh nor talk loud. Old Leaf Buds came to see us. Her husband was going to take care of my father if he was a Killer. And Leaf Buds was going to take care of my mother. So my mother tried to finish the mat she was making, because if my father was a Killer, she would have to be purified and then she could not work at all.

She talked to us while she was finishing her work and told us what to do, because she would be gone four times four days. I was little then and I thought it would be good to stop work for so many days. But some of the women did not like it. They asked their husbands not to be Killers. There was once a woman who was making a big basket and she wanted to get it done. But the men made up a war party. So she told her husband she was menstruating and he had to stay home. They say that woman never menstruated again.

The men were gone eight days. I know how that fight was because my father told me. We were not women who were afraid of war power. We were Killers' women.

The men from all the villages met at Basket Cap Mountain, and there my father made them speeches, sitting with his arms folded and talking low as all great men do. Then they sang the war songs:

Oh, bitter wind, keep blowing
That therewith my enemy
Staggering forward
    Shall fall.

Oh, bitter wind, keep blowing
That therewith my enemy
Staggering sideways
    Shall fall.

Many, many songs they sang but I, a woman, cannot tell you all. I know that they made the enemy blind and dizzy with their singing and that they told the gopher to gnaw their arrows. And I know that they called on our dead warriors who have turned into owls and live in the Apache country to come and tell them where the enemy were. Facing the enemy they sat, while they sang, that they might bring darkness upon him.

All that time the medicine man sat alone on a little hill waiting for the owl-dead to come to him. He had dreamed of owls himself and so he could speak with them. They always took an Owl-Meeter on to war with them to call the dead who are our spies.

Soon that medicine man came back to the others and said, "Has anyone some of our old, wild tobacco?" They gave him some. Then he went back and they saw lights when he made two cigarettes. They saw those lights move as cigarettes do when two people are smoking. They heard the medicine man talking, very low, and then saw both cigarettes thrown away. The medicine man came back and said, "The enemy are at Smooth Ground. We will come up with them at noon tomorrow."

So they did. They jumped on the enemy and fought. When our men go toward an Apache, they do not just walk. They leap. My father got separated from the others, he and one Apache. There was a giant cactus between them. You know a cactus trunk is as wide as a thin man. Each shot at the other, and the other dodged behind the cactus till it was stuck full of arrows to the height of a man.

They could both talk a little Spanish, so they shouted at each other. The Apache said, "I am a *man*." My father: "I, also, a *man!*" They threw down their bows and arrows and started wrestling. My father was down. Far away, his brother saw that and came running. He clubbed the Apache from behind. My father got up and clubbed, too. So he was dead and my father and his brother were Enemy Slayers.

They stopped fighting right away because an enemy's death lets power loose. You must take care of yourself until you have tamed that power or it will kill you. You could not stand against arrows with such power around you. You would be like a sick man. You would fall. So they painted their faces black to show what had happened. They carried black paint for that in little deerskin bags. They stood away from the others, and other men who had killed came to join them.

The leader of the fight saw and he sent an old man who had killed, himself, so that he was not in danger. That man kept them away from the other men the way you keep away people who have a sickness. He made them walk behind the others and camp away from them all the way home. They never mixed their cornmeal for themselves. He mixed it for them—oh, so very little. Brave men do not want to eat when they are getting power. He spoke to them, telling them how they would dream. I do not know what he said to them. Old men know that—old Killers. Even a Slayer's woman like me is not told. But my father told me the end of every speech he made because it was always the same:

> Verily, who desires this thing?
> Do not you desire it?
> Then learn to endure hardship.

One morning we heard shouting. It was the messengers from the war party, two men who had been sent ahead on the fastest horses. They were far outside the village, standing up in their stirrups and yelling:

> One Ear ——— has killed!
> Ridge Face ——— has killed!
> The Gambler ——— has killed!

The last one was my father. They called the name of his brother too, but it was words you white people do not like to say, about peoples' bodies.

We heard them far off, over and over again in a loud sing-song, and everyone came outside to listen to know if we now belonged to the families of Enemy Slayers.

My mother had a basket of corn kernels in her hand; she was going to grind flour. But when she heard the shout she set it down and just stood there. Then Leaf Buds came running to our house. She just motioned to my mother to come with her. My mother did not speak to us, and she did not take anything with her; just her cotton blanket to put over her head, because the wife of a man who is being purified must not see the sun. The husband of Leaf Buds was building a shelter for my mother, out away from the houses. He had to run to do it as soon as he heard the shouts. Until it was done, my mother went to Leaf Buds' house and sat there with her blanket over her head, not speaking. They did not make us children do anything, because children cannot stand the suffering of being purified. But my grandmother called us into the house and told us to stay quietly there. She gave us sticks to scratch our heads with so we would not use our hands and make our hair fall out. She told us not to speak much and never to go near the fire.

So we could not go out to see the men come in. The young girls whose men were not Enemy Slayers ran out to meet the fighters, far into the mountains. Ah, that is a good dance. I did it myself, at other times when there was no Power in the family. The girls stand across the warriors' path and take their weapons from them. They take arrows and quivers and bows, yes, clubs and shields. And they dance with them in front of the men. They dance and they sing with those weapons, and they will not give them back until the men have paid them.

We heard those girls run out, the girls who could run far. And when the men came near we saw the old woman go dancing out; the woman who takes the scalps. Foamy Water was her name; a woman who could not menstruate and hurt those powerful things. She took it when she was old enough from her mother who was called Painted Girl, because Painted Girl was so old she could not dance any more.

But Foamy Water danced hard. They gave her the hair of the Apache, not scalps, just long hairs from the temples, and they gave her his beaded buckskin shoe. They had tied those things on a pole, and she came dancing with it into the village, dancing at every house. She came outside our house making the pole go up and down. She sang:

> Here I stand, singing for my prisoner
> Come and see, Oh, women!
> I dreamed that I saw light
> At the tips of the warriors' feathers.

Then she stuck the pole in front of the council house and all the people went there to hear about the fight. It is the two messengers who tell that story before the fighters come, and sometimes after they tell about the killing, they end up, "But they got some of our men." Then they tell how they made a fire and burned up the dead men with everything they had. Because we dare not bury a man who died in the enemy country. We must have fire to take away the power of the Apache.

We thought if anyone was dead we would hear the crying. So my grandmother listened; she knew the women's voices. But there was no crying. So my grandmother cooked us our food, and she did not put any salt in it, because we were being purified. I sat by the house wall away from the fire and I was cold. I heard the men who had not killed come into the village, yelling and whipping their horses, and I heard everybody singing at the council house, stamping up and down:

> Poor crow. There it hangs. Poor crow.

They sang that way every night for all the days of purifying. It is a good thing to have the enemy's hair raised on a pole above our houses. It calls the clouds to it and brings rain on our land, and then the corn comes up. But those who have brought the blessing cannot dance. Not they and not their families. Leaf Buds' husband went out to meet my father and led him to a mesquite tree far away so that his power would not come near us. He hung his bow and arrows on that tree, and my father sat down under it. So! Do you see? With legs under him and his head on his breast. So our powerful men always sit waiting for a vision. And visions always came to my father.

> I did not know
> I did not know
> And then I knew.

That was what he sang, all alone in the night.

> Alas!
> Something I know
> Clearly I know
> I killed an Apache woman
> She was crying.

> And now light has come to me.

That is the song the Killers have sung since the first one killed an enemy woman. It says that the light has come and told them how to purify themselves.

We did not go near my father. That would have made us sick. And we could not go near my mother in her shelter of branches. But we used to run behind the house and watch when she came out once or twice a day with the sheet over her head so the sun should not see her.

We saw Leaf Buds working all the time making pots. She was a good potter. That was one reason my father had chosen her husband to take care of him, for many bowls are used while a person is being purified. Leaf Buds made new clay bowls, and in one of them she took pinole to my mother, and her husband took another to my father. Every four days the bowl had to be thrown away because it had too much of the power, and she had to have a new one ready. That was the woman who worked hard! She had to make two great jars, new so that they would keep the water cool, and in them she and her husband had to bathe my mother and father every four days. They poured that water over their heads while they sat still, arms folded. It takes a great deal to wash off that power and make it fit to use.

My grandmother bathed us children. She came with the jar at dawn and I ran away around the house. It was cold. She caught me and made me sit facing the west with my arms folded, just like my father. Then she poured it over my head and said, "Now you'll be early rising and industrious. You'll go early for water and wood." She poured it over my brothers too, and said to them, "Now you'll be a good runner, a hunter, able to stand cold and hunger. A Killer!" Those are the things that come to us, the families of the powerful.

The rest of our family were getting ready for the dance. All the old Enemy Slayers were going to sing for my father to take him back again when the four times four days were over. My grandmother boiled big pots of dried corn and dried squash and succotash, to give those singers food. All my father's sisters and the wives of his brothers made tortillas. The young women of our family brought wood for the dance fire. My father's brothers counted how many cows and horses

*Pottery making. Photograph by author, reproduced with the aid of The Denver Museum of Natural History Anthropology Department.*

they could give to the dancers. Our family did not have much because our men were always fighting. They were brave.

At sunset, when the four times four days were over, the people came to the dance place. Then they brought my father and the Enemy Slayers and us, too. They did not take us to the fire. Far away in the cold they dug four little holes and there the Slayers sat, facing east. Behind them there were holes for their wives. They must sit up all night, straight and not move. They had stakes driven into the ground behind them so they could lean back a little when they were too tired. My grandmother sat with us children far away in the dark.

The people went around the fire singing:

> Kill the Apache, kill the Apache!
> Dry the skin, dry the skin!
> Soften it, soften it!
> Hang it up, hang it up!
> A-a-a-a-a-a-h!
> There are still some Apaches left.

I could not hear the songs that night when my father was a Slayer but I know them now, for I learn well. I learn everything that the men sing.

The people stopped going around, and a man came into the middle to dance the warrior's dance. Only a young man can do that dance. He holds the shield and a club, and first he leaps to one side and then to the other as though the enemy's arrows were flying at him. Then he leaps up and lets them pass under him. Behind him, other young men, or maybe women, if they are strong and wild, take bows and arrows and leap as he does. The singers sing for them.

> Sitting with my back against the dawn
> I got drunk, my younger brothers.
> I met the white wind and it drove me mad.

Four young men danced. To each, one of my father's brothers came up and put a piece of manure into his hand. First it was from a cow and then another cow, and then a horse and another horse. That was what my family gave to men who leaped in the war dance. It made them (my family) poor.

Then the old warriors began to sing for the Slayers, because the Pleiades had come to the top of the sky and it was midnight. They sang very secret songs that had come to them when they themselves were purified. Then they lit a long cane cigarette, such as our people used to use, and went and blew the smoke over the new Slayers. They spoke to them as relatives, taking them back again. "Hail, my younger brother. Hail, my nephew. Thus I do to you. You will be like me. You will be a great Killer. You will always find the enemy. You will be hunger-enduring, cold-enduring, thirst-enduring. Thus you will live well." I could not see all this. They made me stay in the dark with my grandmother. But my father told me afterward, for I am a woman to whom a man can tell solemn words and she will remember them well.

Then they took my father out in the dark before the morning came and bathed him again, and they bathed us, too. Then we were purified and we could have the Apache scalp in our family to work for us like a relative. All the time that my father was being purified a woman had been making a basket, the kind that we use only for scalps and other sacred things. My father's guardian had taken the Apache hair and made it into a little man. He could touch Apache hair because he was a Slayer and it would not make him sick.

That little man had a buckskin shirt with fringe, like an Apache, and a feather in its hair and little moccasins. The guardian brought it to my father in the basket. My father was not afraid of that enemy's hair. He said to it, "My child." Then he gave it to my mother and she took it in her arms and said, "My child." He gave it to my brothers and my sisters and me. We held it and said, "My younger brother." Then it was in our family and it would always help us. My father laid it in the basket and all around it he put eagle feathers which are powerful. He put in tobacco and he said, "This is your house, my child." Then he wrapped that basket in deerskins and hung it in the thatch and we had Power.

### III

My younger brother was going to be a medicine man. We knew it from the time he was very little, because sometimes he would fall over as if he was dead. Sitting in the house with us, he would fall over. Or when he was out in the desert, running, he would drop and lie for an hour or two. Sometimes it happened two or three times between one full moon and another.

When it began happening my father and mother called in a medicine man to find out what was the matter. The medicine man only looked at him and blew smoke over him. Then he said, "Let him alone. He is all right. He is learning." So my father and mother were glad. My grandfather had been a medicine man. He had said when he was dying that none of his children would dream as he had but that his grandchildren would. And they did. Yes, I, too. After that we would hear my brother singing at night when we were all lying on our mats. He never told us where he got his songs. But we knew that, when he was dead like that, he met some animal and the animal taught him. Sometimes when a medicine man was singing in our house, my little brother sang with him.

Many medicine men used to come to our house, for we were often sick. In the hungry time before the rains, it used to happen to us. Once, when I was little, we had the owl sickness. My father, my mother, my brothers, and sisters, and I all had it together. We felt sleepy and dizzy and as if our hearts were shaking. We knew it came from the owl, because it always does, but we sent for the medicine man to make sure. Do you do the same?

He came in the evening and my father had tobacco ready for him. He sat and talked for a little while, gossiping about his family, and my father and mother talked with him while we children lay on our sleeping mats. Then he began to sing. It was dark except for the fire and I could just see the rattle going to and fro in his right hand, the way a dog switches its tail. To and fro for the first two songs, up and down for the second two. You cannot tell what a medicine man sings. He sings his dreams and he sings them in a voice that is not like a man's. It takes him many years to learn that strange voice. But at the fourth song sometimes he sings real words and you know what animal came to visit him and taught him.

After the fourth song he smoked a cigarette made in a joint of reed long as my hand, as old cigarettes used to be. He put his hand on our bodies while he smoked to feel the sickness, and he listened and looked out in the dark. I was not frightened when he put his hand on me. My mother had said to me beforehand, "The medicine man will do what he knows and you must not be scared." So I went to sleep.

But my father and mother sang with him all night. He sang one song so often that they learned it. And my little brother sang, too. After every fourth song he smoked a whole cigarette.

Then he took out the crystals which he had to see by. Those are crystals which a man keeps inside his breast. They are little shining things, as long as a finger joint but they cast light like a fire. Some medicine men dream where to find them and they go out in the bare mountains and see them lying there, burning in the sun. Then they swallow them and keep them safe in their hearts. But some men never have to find them. Their crystals grow inside them as a worm can grow. Even if you suck it out, still it grows again. Those are the men who have great power.

Our medicine man had crystals which he had picked up, but he told my father that when he swallowed them, they leaped into his mouth out of his hand and went down his throat like water. He never took them out again because he could see even while they were in his body. While he was sitting there in the house he could see things going on outside and inside, too. Even if someone was coming far away, he could see. At dawn he said to my father, "It's this way. The owls are making you sick."

My father gave him a heifer because we always paid the medicine men well, and then we had to sing away the owls. When an animal is making you sick like that, you sing many songs about him to make him feel better. Any kind of songs. Songs that make you laugh and songs that tell where he lives and songs that say mean things about him. The animal does not care. He likes to be sung about.

People had to be sent for who had dreamed of owls, because that is how all songs come, by dreaming. Owl songs are pretty and even women can dream them. Many owl singers came to our house, and all the neighbors crowded in to listen:

> Evening is growing red.
> Straight above me the color spreads out
> In all directions.
> I fly out and hoot at it
> Four times.

I learned that song. Later on I dreamed of owls, too. When they sang I felt very peaceful; I knew things would be all right. The singers brushed me off with owl feathers and I went to sleep. At midnight my mother gave them a big meal of succotash and at dawn they went away. In two days we were well.

I used to try to sing owl songs after that. It seemed to me that I was always just going to dream about an owl. But I am not sure if I did.

Every winter there was singing in our house. We had the deer sickness, which makes you swell, and Hit-with-the-Heel came to sing the deer songs. Or we had the turtle sickness which makes you sore, or someone stepped over a snake and we had the snake sickness which makes you vomit. I know those songs. Many nights I lay on my mat, hearing them each one four times, eight times, sixteen times. Some women are thinking only of baskets and they do not remember such things. But I remember.

Once I got sick myself. It was from my father's scalps, they said. My father had been a Slayer three times by then and in our house there was a basket with four Apache dolls. Prisoners, we call them. My father would send us all out of the house, and he would take down that basket and talk to them. "Now, my children, I am going to give you tobacco. Now, my children, here is a little food for you." Then he would give them some of the good squash we had just taken from our field.

But somehow he must have angered them, so that they felt they were not treated well. Those Prisoners are very wild. They come out of their basket like little men and run about the house at night. It happens even if you do not make them into dolls as my father's guardian did—even if you simply lay the hair in a basket. They come like handsome men and lie beside women and make them sick. They pinch you and pull your hair at night, or they swing up and down in their basket and whistle. Sometimes a man comes home to see a handsome young man coming out of his house. He goes in angry to his wife, and she says there has been no one there. It was the scalp. Then the owner must give it eagle feathers and speak kindly to it. These Prisoners are dangerous.

They did not come like a man to me, but my head ached, I vomited. I ached all over. The medicine man sang and smoked all night, and then he said, "It's the Prisoners."

The only thing to do was for men who had taken scalps to come and sing for me the songs they had dreamed when they were being purified. There were four Slayers in our village. They were Spider Hole, Squirrel Ear, Yellow Legs, and one had just a Mexican name, José.

They came in the evening. My sleeping mat was moved up close to the fire and they sat around me. Each had four down feathers from under the tail of an eagle fastened to a little stick. That is one of the most sacred things we have, those eagle down feathers, because they bring the rain; they almost *are* the rain. All men who have Prisoners have those feathers to keep their Prisoners quiet.

They took their feathers out of little deerskin bags, and then took gourd rattles in their right hands. I like to hear a gourd rattle; it makes me want to dance. But it cures the sick, too. It is a great thing.

First Spider Hole rattled, and sang four songs that had come to him in his loneliness after he had killed an enemy. Then he blew over me and he cleaned me with the eagle's feathers, brushing them over me. Then all the others blew and cleaned me, too. Then Squirrel Ear sang four songs and then they brushed again. I went to sleep. But they sang and cleansed me all night and my father smoked and sang with them, because he was an Enemy Slayer. Women must not sing those songs, so my mother sat and listened, and at midnight she brought them beans and succotash. They sang the last song at dawn and then they went away.

I began to feel better as soon as they started singing. I had not slept for two days, but I slept that night. In two days I was well.

But I used to dream after that. Sometimes I would think I saw the little men, the Prisoners, climbing down the house posts out of their basket and looking at me. They would point to their mouths and ask for food because, perhaps, my father had not fed them enough. Sometimes, when I was in the desert digging roots, I would see the centipedes and the little red spiders talking together, planning how to make rain. Just after daybreak I would see a coyote darting past the house and I would know he had come to see me.

I knew all about Coyote and the things he can do, because my father told us the stories about how the world began and how Coyote helped our Creator, Elder Brother, to set things in order. Only some men know these stories, but my father was one of them. On winter nights, when we had finished our gruel or rabbit stew and lay back on our mats, my brothers would say to him, "My father, tell us something."

My father would lie quietly upon his mat with my mother beside him and the baby between them. At last he would start slowly to tell us about how the world began. This is a story that can be told only in winter when there are no snakes about, for if the snakes heard they would crawl in and bite you. But in winter when snakes are asleep, we tell these things. Our story about the world is full of songs, and when the neighbors heard my father singing they would open our door and step in over the high threshold. Family by family they came, and we made a big fire and kept the door shut against the cold night. When my father finished a sentence we would all say the last word after him. If anyone went to sleep he would stop. He would not speak any more. But we did not go to sleep.

My father's story told us about why we hold our big feasts, because Elder Brother showed us how in the beginning of the world. My father went to those feasts and he took us, too, because my father was a song maker and he had visions, even if he was not a medicine man. He always made a song for the big harvest festival, the one that keeps the world going right and that only comes every four years.

We all went then, from all over our country to the Place of the Burnt Seeds. We camped together, many, many families together, and we made images of the beautiful things that make life good for the Desert People, like clouds and corn and squash and deer. The men sang about those things and my father made songs. When I was about eight years old, my father once made an image of a mountain out of cactus ribs covered with white cloth. He had dreamed about that mountain and this is the song he made:

> There is a white shell mountain in the ocean
> Rising half out of the water.
> Green scum floats on the water
> And the mountain turns around.

The song is very short because we understand so much. We can understand how tall and white the mountain was, and that white shell is something precious, such as the handsome men of old used to have for their necklaces, and it would shine all across the earth as they walked. We understand that as that mountain turns, it draws the clouds and the birds until they all float around it. All those things my father told me when he used to sing that song in our house. I did not understand, though, when I was a little girl and went to the harvest festival. I was afraid of the singers with their masks. There were clowns with masks, too, white masks with little holes for eyes. The clowns bless people, and one put his hand out to bless me, but I ducked under it and ran.

Only afterward I used to dream of the white clown. Perhaps it was because some day I was going to marry one. It may be, for I have magic dreams. I am one who understands things.

When we came home that year there was sickness at Mesquite Root. It was a bad sickness that came to everybody in the whole village, sent by an evil medicine man. We all had it: my father, my mother, all my brothers and sisters. The singers gathered in the big house and sang. You understand now that our way to cure everything and to take care of everything is to sing.

Then the medicine men took branches of a kind of cholla cactus. Oh, very thorny that cactus is, covered with white thorns, and people say they jump out at you and catch you, so hard they stick. Everything in the world sticks to that cactus, so we say the sickness will stick to it, too. The medicine men went with their branches into every house, gathering up the sickness on those thorns. I remember, because I was not so sick as the others, how little boys came after them, making fun of them and waving greasewood branches. But we do not mind those things. We know the children do not understand. They took the sickness away and buried it at the north of the village.

My little brother sang a great deal in the house after those things happened. Of course he could not tell us what he was dreaming because that would spoil his power. But I will tell you what he did, long after that, when all knew he could cure. Some men were at our house and they were laughing at him. They said, "You cannot be a medicine man. What can you do?"

My brother stooped down and drew a ring on the ground. Then he picked up some smooth little pebbles that were lying there on the desert. He spit on the stones, pff! and threw one up into the air. It fell in the circle and it looked as though a baby quail was hatching out of an egg. We saw its eyes and its bill; it was wobbling and trying to run. He spit on the other stone, pff! and threw it up. It fell in the circle and there was another quail. The two went fluttering around the circle. Then he took them up one by one, spit on them, and they were stones again.

I could not go into the desert like my brother. I had no time; I had to work. But in those days I used to see things around me that no one else saw. Once a song came to me. I cannot tell you when it came but I think it was when I was very little. You see, I come of a singing family. It is natural for us to see strange things and to make songs. This came when I had been sick once. I was lying still in the house with everybody gone, and I dreamed that Coyote came to me as he must have come to my brother so many times. I saw him lying asleep on the desert, though I was in the house. Then I saw him get up, shake himself a little and look at me. Then he sang:

> Very sleepy
> Yonder he slept
> Then getting up
> He sang to me
> Ai-i-i!
> I sway to and fro
> To and fro.

I used to sing that around the house, but not the words. I just made noises. I knew one must not tell if he had seen Coyote. But I saw other things, too. I would see a spider on the central post of the house, who stopped and looked at me, just ready to speak. And in the desert, when I saw a little gray horned toad just in front of my foot, it looked at me as though it understood something.

I was always running about in those days, looking at these things, acting strange. My mother saw it and she did not think it was right. She told me to keep to my work, for I was nearly old enough to grind the corn. Then once we went to the Cleared Land to visit a brother of my grandmother. My father asked him to sing over me to see what was the matter. He sang all night, and in the morning he said, "You could be a medicine woman." "That cannot be," said my father. "We have one medicine man in the house and it is enough." So the medicine man said he would take out my crystals. He leaned over me and sucked them out of my breast, one by one. They were as long as the joint of my little finger, white and moving a little. He said, "Look, I have taken them out before they got big." Then he made a hole in a giant cactus and put them inside. Then he looked at me and said, "They will grow again, for it is a gift."


## IV

In the summer everyone came home to our village and we planted corn. The corn was once a man and he lured a woman away to sleep with him. She stayed a long time, and when she came home, she knew the songs that made the corn grow. So when the men all went to their meeting, this man did not go but he stayed at home hearing his wife sing. The men from the meeting came to speak to him. "Why are you absent?" "Because I am listening to my wife." "How can it be that a man can learn more from a woman than from talking with us? Let us hear her, too."

So she came to the men's meeting and she sat between the chief and her husband. "Sing." And she sang the corn songs.

At the first song those men began to sing. At the second, they danced. At the third, the women came out of the houses, creeping to the council house to listen to the singing. At the fourth, they were all dancing, inside the council house and outside, to that woman's singing.

We sang those songs as we put the corn into the earth, but it was the men who sang, for women do not do those things now. We stood ready with the corn kernels while the men sang, then we went down the field together, each woman behind a man. The man dropped his stick into the soft earth, thud! As deep as my hand is long. The woman dropped in four corn kernels and scraped her bare toes over that red earth to cover them.

Then the corn came up. The fair stalks, the thick root, the broad leaves.

> I saw the tassels waving in the wind
> And I whistled softly for joy.

My father used to sing that at night while the corn was growing.

I used to like it in the summertime when all our friends and relatives were around us. The houses were scattered all over the flat land—round brush houses like ours. In every house there were women grinding corn, and down by the wash there were men bending over the fields where the corn and beans and squash were growing.

> In the furrow
> At the corner
> The corn is growing green
> Growing green.

I used to hear those songs coming from the houses, because we were so happy in summertime. We had rain. Every morning the sky was bright and every after-noon the little white cloud stood over the mountains to the east. Everywhere by the washes you saw the centipedes that are a sign of rain. We call them a blessing, those centipedes. There were so many that you could shake your head and, pff! one would fall out of your hair. Now there are no more. That fine weather is gone.

We women did not have to fetch water. We could sit in the house and make baskets. Or else we could go off over the land to pick the fine fresh green things. At sunset all the village was full of laughing people, eating around their home fires.

Then we heard the crier call, "Come hither! Bring your cigarettes. We will smoke and talk of what we shall do!"

That call was for the men, not for the women. They got up from the fires and we saw them passing in the starlight against the gray desert that looks almost white on summer nights. I know what my father used to say to them in that meeting, for he has often told me how they spoke after the cigarette went round.

"Well! will you be ready? Take care, for often I have warned you. You must make arrows and your bow you must have in readiness, for when the enemy will arrive, you do not know. At night he may come; at night or in the morning or when the sun stands anywhere in the sky. Then you will arise, your bow you will snatch and therewith will fight the enemy.

"Close by you must keep your bow, your quiver, your hardwood arrows, and your reed arrows with the stone tip. Early in the morning must you have your food that you may be able to fight the enemy. Your girls very early must cook and must give food to the youths that they may be strong to fight no matter where the sun stands in the sky. Your girls shall pour water and shall search for wood and shall cook food. Early in the morning your girls shall run that when the enemy shall come, they can run swiftly and can save their lives.

"This I feel and this I say. Listen and my words shall enter your ears and enter your heads."

So he talked to them, and then they spoke of whether they would widen the ditches and if the boys were practicing well for the races, and maybe a man from some other village was there to tell them the news. There was not a man among us who would miss that meeting.

We women sat in the dark, under the shelter, and told about the strange things we had heard. We told how there is a root which men carry to make the deer come to them and it makes women come, too. It smells strong and sweet, and you can smell it on the sweaty hands of a man beside you in the dance. If it is very strong and has been used in many love matches, sometimes it turns into a man. It walks up beside a woman while she is sleeping and makes her dream.

We told how, in our village, a girl was struck by lightning. Someone must have been menstruating and not have confessed it, said the medicine man. So he called all the girls, took out his crystals and looked at them. "It was the girl herself," he said. "She has killed herself."

We told how, when a woman does not seem to care for any man or a man for any woman, that person is really married to a snake. There was a man in our village who used to go out alone into the desert and disappear in a wash. His parents followed him and found there a little red snake with her baby snakes on her back. They said to their son, "What! have you a family of snakes?" He said, "No, she is a beautiful woman." That is how snakes fool you. The older women used to tell us, too, that if we thought too much about any boy before we were married, that boy would seem to come to make love to us. But it would not be he, it would only be a snake. So girls must not think too much about boys. That was what the old women told us. We must not think about boys and we must not talk to boys. When we were married it would be time enough to speak to a man. Now it was better to work and be industrious.

So I worked. But I used to think while I was sitting under the shelter with my basketry, about whether I would get a good man and whether I would like being married. I used to hear a good deal about married peoples' troubles, because my father was chief in Mesquite Root. Married people who had quarrels brought their troubles to him. There was a post in front of our house where people were beaten who did wrong, and all the village would come to see and talk about what happened.

Once I remember how a wife came, very angry. She had walked a long way to tell about her husband. "He beats me," she said to my father. "You who are One Made Big Over Us, he beats me! But I love him." My father used to smile at things like that. He was a warrior and a gambler. He did not care about beating women. But he always settled things for them. So he sent for the husband. "Do you beat her?" "Yes," said the man. He was a young man. I remember how he looked at the woman, his wife, while he stood there. "Yes, I beat her. But I want her with me. I'm jealous. I beat her because I think she looks at other men." "I don't look at other men," said the woman, crying. So her husband said very quickly: "Oh, I want her back. It's all right." "Will you stop beating her?" "Yes, yes." The woman said, "But he has beaten me already. Many times and for nothing. Let him pay me." "How?" "With his body," said the woman. "Let him be beaten as I was beaten." My father thought about that and he said, "All right. How many stripes?" "Fifty." "You want to kill him," said my father. "I'll make it twenty." So the man knelt down and took off his shirt. The chief did not beat wrongdoers himself. He had a messenger who was called the Chief's Leg. That Leg was a man who meant much to me later on. He took the rawhide whip to beat the man, but he did not raise too many welts. Men are sorry for each other.

Another time a father came with his daughter. "This girl will not lie with the man to whom I gave her." My father looked at the new husband who had come, too, and he thought he seemed a good man. "Is it true?" my father said to the girl. "Don't you want this man?" "Yes, it's true I'm afraid." "Well, we'll beat you. Then you can decide." So they tied her hands and the girl whimpered, "I'll take him." "Take her by the hand," my father told the husband, "and lead her home. If she misbehaves, come back."

I thought about that girl sometimes and I thought I would have been afraid, too. Then I asked my mother, though I did not tell her how I was feeling. My mother said, "It's right to be afraid of men. All good girls are."

We girls never saw men except our brothers. And our brothers kept away from us now we were almost maidens. They said that sometime we might become maidens suddenly and then if they touched anything that we had touched, it would take away their strength. So the boys did not play with us any more.

But I used to think about boys when I was—let me see, we do not count our ages—thirteen. Sometimes I thought I heard flutes at night. I do not know if it was really boys playing them or if I only dreamed it. But the music drove me wild. The flute is what our boys play when they want a woman to come to them and I wanted to go.

But my father said to me, "Never talk to a man alone. If one comes to the house when there is no one there but you, then offer him food. If he is a relative, say, 'Wait till I cook you something.' Even if he is a stranger, say, 'You had better eat.' But do not talk while you feed him. And if you have nothing in the house tell him quickly so he will go away and not wait, expecting."

So I did that way and so did the other girls, all except a few wild ones. When we went to the hills to gather fruits, we went all together and an old woman with us. When we went to the pond with jars on our heads to get water, we went in a group. Sometimes there would be boys there watering their horses. The wild girls would throw gravel at them, then laugh and run. I never did that.

I was a good housekeeper. I did all the cooking and I fetched the water and ground the corn. I could catch the horses, too, and saddle them for my brothers. But I could not go out alone on the desert as they did. Why should I want to? That is man's work and no woman with a right heart wants to be a man. But I was excitable. My heart was not cool. When I had finished my work, I always wanted to race, and I was a good racer—the fastest of all the girls. And I was a gambler. Yes, always I have been a gambler and a lucky one. When I had ground the corn and fetched the firewood for the day, I used to run out to the houses where my girl cousins lived: "Come on. Let's throw dice."

We had dice which we made of sticks, painted black on one side with charcoal from the fire. Every girl had four, and we kept them always with us as we kept our red paint. We sat in a circle, and all the people gathered to watch us and bet on the game. Each girl in turn tapped her sticks on a stone and threw them. Two points if all black, one if all white. And if of different colors, let the next girl throw!

We bet everything on that game. I had baskets which I had made and a mat. My father had brought me shell beads from the River Country and all those things I wagered. My mother did not mind; she was looking on. She would not say a word if I bet everything I had, even my clothes. But I never bet her things or my sisters'. Neither did my father. He bet his own things and he gambled all the time. That was his name, the Gambler.

Once I played against a grown woman from another village. First, I won her red woven girdle, then a whole red dress, then a Mexican scarf. She went back to her house and got everything she had—a basket, a mat, a big water jar. She said she wanted to bet them all, but she would race me on the race track.

So we went to the track and all the people came with us, betting. We chose two men to take charge: a relative of mine for the starter, one of hers for the finisher. I started from one end, she from the other and all the people yelled. But then hers stopped yelling and mine went on. She was not winning. I reached her relatives who stood at the end of the track where she started, and she was still far from the rope. Her relative had to make mine stop yelling and then he said I had won. I heard her crying that night in the desert because she had lost everything.

My father was a gambler, too. He used to go all over our country playing against the men. Beads and necklaces he used to bring me back from the River People. And sometimes he took all the family with him when there were races between the villages and all our young men ran. But he would not let me run at those races nor bet on them.

"Wait till you are married," he said. "When you have a husband he will take you to the feasts. They are for married people, not for young girls."

He would not let me go to any feasts at all, not even to the maidens' dances, when they happened in our own village and to my own cousins. When a maiden came of age, the people sometimes danced every night until the moon got back to where it was when they began. The men and women danced with their arms over each other's shoulders. We wore nothing on our bodies above the waist then. The young men liked that. It is said that some young girls did not come home at night. It is said that some babies were dropped in the arroyo and no one knew.

They told me that there were women who went alone to those dances, the wild women, who did not work and who went about painted every day. Corn ears they painted on their breasts, and birds and butterflies, each breast different for the men to see. And a woman's breast, in that dance, comes just where a man's hand can reach it.

I began to dream of those wild women. They can haunt you just as the Prisoners do. They make men and women crazy, sometimes so that they run out and die. Then you must make little clay dolls, a man and a woman, and have the medicine man sing over them to quiet the sick person. I was not bad enough for that, but sometimes, when I sat alone at my basketry, it would seem to me that I saw a boy and a girl making love and it made me wild.

And I dreamed strange things. Once my mother sent me after water and I was all alone; the other girls had gone earlier in the day. I had to cross a dry wash. As I came up to it, there I saw a snake three times as thick as a man. That wash was full of caves, and the snake's head was in one of them, his tail in another, with his body stretched all across the wash. When I tried to cross it, he would hit me on the legs. I ran home without the water and my father was angry. My mother came with me to see what was the matter and there was no snake there.

And I kept hearing flutes; flutes in the morning and evening. Such lovely music that I would stand still in the house to listen. I thought my crystals were growing again.

V

When I was nearly as tall as my mother, that thing happened to me which happens to all our women though I do not know if it does to the whites; I never saw any signs. It is called menses.

Girls are very dangerous at that time. If they touch a man's bow, or even look at it, that bow will not shoot any more. If they drink out of a man's bowl, it will make him sick. If they touch the man himself, he might fall down dead. My mother had told us this long ago and we knew what had happened in our village.

There was a girl once who became dangerous and she did not tell. They were having a good time that day. All the village was planting in her father's field, and he had given them a meal of succotash. They were eating out in the field, her mother was cooking over a campfire. My mother was there and she said this girl was standing with a bowl in the crook of her arm, laughing and eating. It began to rain. The girl and her sisters ran home to take in the bedding, because we sleep out of doors in the summer and it was on the ground.

There was a crash of thunder. All the eating people stood still and then, from the house of that girl they heard a long sigh. They ran there. All the family were lying stunned on the floor, one sister was blind, and that girl was dead. The men dragged the people out into the rain and the house began to burn. "See," said those people, "what has happened to us." Her relatives buried that girl all alone and no one would go near.

Then there was a girl who was going to build a fire, and it seemed that it reached out, and took her, and burned her up. And there was another whose mother was struck by lightning. For it is not always you who are hurt if you commit this sacrilege; it may be any one in your family.

That is why, when the lightning strikes a village, they send for the medicine man to see what woman was dangerous. He summons all the girls and looks at his crystals to see who did it. They do not punish that woman. It is enough to know that she has killed her friends.

Our mothers watch us, and so mine knew when it came to me. We always had the Little House ready, over behind our own house. It was made of some

*Menstruation hut. Photograph by author.*

branches stuck in the ground and tied together at the top, with greasewood thrown over them to make it shady. There was no rain then, for it was winter, but it was cold in that little house. The door was just big enough to crawl through, like our house door, and there was room for you to lie down inside, but not to stand up. My mother made me a new bowl and drinking cup out of clay, and put them in that house. When my mother cooked food at the big house, she would come over and pour some in my bowl, but no meat and nothing with salt in it. My father sharpened a little stick for me to scratch my hair with, because if I touched it, it would fall out. I was so afraid to lose my nice long hair that I kept that stick in my mouth all the time. Even when I was asleep, I had it there.

It is a hard time for us girls, such as the men have when they are being purified. Only they give us more to eat, because we are women. And they do not let us sit and wait for dreams. That is because we are women, too. Women must work.

They chose my father's cousin to take care of me. She was the most industrious woman we had, always running with the carrying basket. That old woman would come for me in the dark when morning-stands-up. "Come," she said. "Let's go for water over across the mountain. Let's go for firewood."

So we would run, far, far across the flat land and up the mountain and bring the water back before daylight. I would leave it outside my father's house and not go in. Then that old woman would talk to me.

"Work hard. If you do not work hard now, you will be lazy all your life. Then no one will want to marry you. You will have to take some good-for-nothing man for a husband. But if you are industrious, we shall find you a good old man."

That is what we call our husbands: old man. But this woman did it out of modesty, too, so that I should not have young men in my mind. "When you have an old man," she said, "you will grind the corn for him and you will always have water there for him to drink. Never let him go without water. Never let him go without food. He will go to the house of someone else to eat and you will be disgraced."

I listened to her. Do you say that some girls might think of other things and not listen? But I wanted to be a good woman! And I have been. Ask anyone in our village if they ever saw me with idle hands. Or legs, either, when I was younger.

All the girls came around the Little House while that woman talked. They did not come near, because that would not be safe, and she would call to them, "Go away." But they sat and listened and when she was tired of talking, they laughed and sang with me. And we played a game with little stones and a ball. We pick up the stones in different ways with one hand while we catch the ball in the other. Oh, we have good times at the Little House, especially when that first month is over. But other women who were dangerous did not come; that would be too much.

I had to stay four days and then I was not dangerous any more. Everything goes by fours with our people, and Elder Brother arranged it that even this thing should be the same. No woman has trouble for more than four days. Then they gave me a bath just as they did to my father. Oh, it was cold in the winter time! I tell the girls who come of age in the summer they do not know what hardship is. The water even feels nice in summer.

My mother came in the dark of the morning with the water in a big new jar. The women had to run all day to get the water ready for me. I tried to get away, but my mother caught me and made me kneel down. Then she dipped a gourd in the jar and poured that cold water down over my forehead.

> Hail!
> I shall pour this over you.
> You will be one who endures cold.
> You will think nothing of it.

It is true, I have never felt cold.

Then my mother washed my hair with soapweed fibers. That is the way women should always wash their hair and it will never grow gray. She cut it so it came just to my shoulders, for we women cannot have hair as long as the men; it would get in our way when we work. But we like to have it thick and shiny, and we know that everybody is noticing. There was quite a lapful that my mother cut off, and she saved it to make hair ropes for our carrying baskets. She had new clothes for me: two pieces of unbleached muslin, tied around my waist with a string. We did not know how to sew in those days. We pinned them together over our hips with bought pins, but it was very modest.

Then I could go back to our house, only still I had to use the stick for four days and I could not eat salt. And then they danced me. All that month they danced me, until the moon got back to the place where it had been at first. It is a big time when a girl comes of age; a happy time. All the people in the village knew that I had been to the Little House for the first time, so they come to our house and the singer for the maidens came first of all.

That singer was the Chief's Leg, the man I told you about. He knew all the songs, the ones that Elder Brother first sang when he used to go over the country, dancing all the maidens. That Leg was the man who danced every maiden in our village when she came of age. His wife danced opposite him. She was the one who was to get the hair that my mother had cut off. He had another wife, too, but not such a good dancer.

"Come out," said my father on that first night. "Now you must dance or the Leg will drag you out. He's mean."

I did not want to dance; I was sleepy and I had run so far. Always when I had heard the others singing those maiden songs, from far away, I had been wild to go. But now it was my turn and all I wanted to do was sleep. But Luis, the Leg, came into the house and took me by the arm. He always danced next to the maiden, with his arm over her shoulders and the rattle in his other hand. He and I were at one end of a long line of people and his wife at the end of a line opposite. There was first a boy and then a girl, all down the line, with their arms over each other's shoulder and the blankets held along at the back. I told you the boys always liked that dance.

The lines went to and fro, toward each other, and they kept wheeling a little, till at last they had made a circle.

> On top of Baboquiviri Peak
> There is a fire burning.
> So near I came.
> I saw it blow all over the ground
> Shining.

> On the flat land
> There is a house of clouds.
> There stand white butterfly wings (of clouds).
> It pleased me. That was what I saw.

Those were the songs they sang, with the rattle going in the night. We had no fire; we kept warm dancing. After every four songs Luis stopped, because his voice was hoarse. Then he let me go, and we girls went and sat together while the men smoked. How dark and cold it was then, with only one ember to light their cigarettes!

There were girls who did not come to sit with us and boys who did not sit with the men. How dark it was! Some mothers went looking for their girls in the night and some did not.

At midnight my mother brought jars of succotash. She had been cooking all day for this dance, and every day after that she cooked and ground corn and baked bread in the ashes. Every morning we gave gifts to Luis and his wife—my cut-off hair and dried beans and cooked food and the hand-woven cotton that I wore for a dress. And to the girl friends who danced beside me, I gave my beads and my baskets because these people had suffered and endured sleeplessness with us.

We stopped dancing in the dark of the morning and then my mother said, "Come and get firewood. Do you want to grow up a lazy woman?" So then I went out in the dark to pick up the dead branches and bring them back before I slept. It seemed I slept only an hour before they were saying, "Get up! Get water. Get wood. Grind the corn. If you sleep at this time you will be sleepy all your life."

Oh, I got thin in that time! We girls are like strips of yucca fiber after our coming of age is over. Always running, and mostly gruel and ash bread to eat, with no salt. And dancing every night from the time the sun sets until morning-stands-up. I used to go to sleep on Luis' arm and he pinched my nose to wake me.

Every night they came, the people who were not too sleepy from the night before. And always the young people came. Even Luis did not know songs enough for all that month and other men sang, too. It is a nice thing for a man to know maidens' songs. Every man likes to dance next to the maiden and to hold her on his arm. But Luis was an old man and his wife danced opposite. The wife always does.

At last the moon had come around again and they gave me a bath. It was over. I looked like half of myself. All my clothes were gone. All our dried corn and beans were eaten up. But I was grown up. Now the medicine man could cleanse me and give me a name.

You have to be cleansed as soon as the month is over; you must not wait. A cousin of mine did that once. She meant to be cleansed but she just waited. I think, perhaps she did not have anything to pay the medicine man. But while she waited, one of her brothers was chopping wood. Something fell on him like a hot coal and killed him. So I went the day after my bath.

My mother and I went to the house of the medicine man early in the morning, with a big basket my mother had made, to pay him. He drew a circle on the ground and made me sit in it, crosslegged, with my back to the rising sun. In front of me he put a little dish. Then he walked away where we could not see him and took something out of a little deerskin bag. It was the clay that he carries to charm the evil away from women. No one ever sees the medicine man dig up that clay and no one knows how he mixes it. But I know, because my brother was a medicine man and because I myself have seen things. He grinds up the bone of a dead man and some owl feathers so that they are fine dust.

He put that clay in a tiny bowl before me, mixed with a little water. Then he walked up and down four times, facing the sun that was behind me. Every time he came up to me he blew over my head and dusted me off with his eagle feathers to brush away the evil. And every time he turned, he made a noise like an owl: hm. The fifth time, he took up the bowl of clay and stirred it around with a little owl feather that was standing in the center of it. Then he put the clay to my mouth. "Drink this up!" So I drank it all.

Then he marked me, the sacred marks that are put on the men who have got salt from the magic ocean; the marks that take away bad luck and bring you a good life. On my breast, on my shoulders, my back, and my belly.

"Your name shall be Cha-veela." I did not know before what name he was going to give me; neither did my parents. The medicine man names one from his dreams. Some of my friends had names that could be understood like Leaf Buds, Rustling Leaves, Windy Rainbow, Dawn Murmur. But I have never understood my name and he did not tell me.

After all that work, I did not menstruate again for a year!

## VI

My father said to me, "Look, my girl. We are going to marry you, over at that house."

He did not say the boy's name out of modesty, just motioned with his lips eastward down the valley. The place he meant was Where the Water Whirls Around, where I went with my clay jars every time our pond went dry. I knew every house there and the people in them. I knew who the marriageable young man was. It was the medicine man's son. I had never spoken to him; I had never spoken to any young men except relatives and of course we do not marry relatives. But my breasts were getting large, now. That is how we know when a girl should marry. "They ought to be used for something," we say.

So my father and mother had been consulting. It must have been when I was asleep at night for I had not heard them. They had decided on a man to ask and then my father had sent my mother to tell my aunts and uncles about it. They all approved. They had not told the boy yet. That is done last of all. But of course no man would refuse, even if he already had a first wife. It would not be polite.

My father went on talking to me in a low voice. That is how our people always talk to their children, so low and quiet the child thinks he is dreaming it. But he never forgets.

'We want you to behave yourself as we have always taught you to. Stay there in the right way. Don't wait for your mother-in-law to tell you what to do. Get up early, find wheat, grind flour. If you can't make tortillas, have flour ready for her to make them. You stay right there and make your home there. It has been here, but now you belong there. Stay home, don't run around. Do your work, carry the wood, cook something, whatever there is. Any work you see, you do it.

"Don't go off to people's houses and walk around and gossip. Gossip may spoil a good home. That husband of yours, listen to him. Don't talk when he's talking, for he is like a chief to you. Don't beg him to take you with him here and there, but if he wants you to go, go whether you feel like it or not. Don't one day get mad at your mother-in-law or father-in-law. Don't think you can get mad and run home. A day will come when your husband will want to visit us and will bring you. Now that's your home and if good luck is with you, you will grow old and die there. This is the way it is. Now I'm going over to tell the boy's father and mother."

So my father went to those people's house, down Where the Water Whirls Around.

"Your son is industrious and I have an industrious daughter. Shall we marry them?"

No one can say anything but yes to such a question. If they really thought the girl was lazy and bad, they would try to be away from home. But they were very distant relatives and, of course, someone had told them what was being talked about. They said, "Very well."

My father told them, "I'm going to see that my daughter behaves herself. You watch her, too, and make sure that she follows my training." They said, "That is what we feel about our son. We have talked to him long enough; he should know his duty. See that he follows it and so will we."

So they sent the boy to our house so that in my first nights with a man I could have my mother near. Before he came, my mother said, "If he wants anything, don't be afraid of him. That's why we are having you marry."

But I was very much afraid. I did not go and hide in the granary basket, the way one of my friends did. That was Rustling Leaves, but she was being married to an old medicine man who had her three sisters as wives already. My husband was a boy, not much older than I and he had no other wives. Only, when I thought of him, fear ran through me like a snake. He used to come to our house after dark, because it would not be modest for him to sit and eat with our family by daylight. And when morning-stood-up he went away. That's how I was married.

When he had been at our house four nights, it was time for me to go home and live with him. He left our house at dawn from modesty, and my mother and I went in the afternoon. My mother had her carrying basket on her back with a jar of cactus syrup as a present. But I took nothing. I left my basketry tools, my dice, and my red face paint, all at my father's house. A bride does not go and get those things until she feels at home in the new place.

We came to Where the Water Whirls Around and stood out behind their house. My mother put down her carrying basket and we waited to be invited in. That is how we do when we go to someone else's house. The door is always open, or if they are under the arbor in summer, there is no door. But we do not walk in. We wait for someone to see us and to say, "There is an arrival."

My mother-in-law came out, took the syrup from my mother's basket, carried it into the house, and put it away. Then she came out with some beans and corn, and filled the carrying basket. She said to me, "I have put the mat for you." So I went into the house and my mother went home, crying in the evening, with that basket of corn and beans.

Their house was a grass house, like ours. At one end of it slept the old people, then two boys who were almost grown up, then two little children, then my husband and I. My mother-in-law came to the mat she had placed there for us and laid on it a waist and a skirt and some beads. I had not had many real waists before that. Pretty soon my husband came in.

He was a strong young man and he was clever. He was going to be a medicine man, only his family did not know it. He was nice to me but I was afraid of him. We had not really talked yet. I sat there and laughed a little but I did not talk, and the next morning I got up and ground the corn. My mother-in-law did not have any grown daughter, only those sons, and she was glad someone had come to do the work. She and I laughed and talked in the house. Only I was afraid of my husband. I had never talked to a man at all and I did not know what to say. Maybe I never would have talked to him; I do not know. Only one night when we went to bed, there was a rattlesnake in our bed. I screamed. He said, "Get up and we'll shake our bedding." After that I felt more at home.

My husband had three brothers. Two of them were big boys, almost ready to be married. One was called Thundering Wings and the other we always called by a nickname, One-on-Top-of-Another. That was because once he went to Mexico and bought two shawls. He did not know how to carry them on the horse, so he tied them both around his shoulders, one on top of another.

Those two brothers were going to be medicine men, only we did not know it yet. Medicine men do not tell their power until they have really begun to cure and these boys were just dreaming. They used to tease me because I was their first sister-in-law and the only girl in the house. I said, "Go and get some wives. I want company."

The third brother was called Shining Evening and he was a man-woman. His parents suspected it when he was very young because he never wanted to play with boys, always with girls. So they thought they would test him. They built a little enclosure and in it they put a bow and arrow and some basketry materials. They told the boy to go in there and play, and when he was busy they set fire to the enclosure. They thought they would see which things he saved. Out he came, carrying the basketry materials. They tried the same thing again and again after that, and it was always the same. The man-woman was very pleasant, always laughing and talking, and a good worker. She was so strong! She did not get tired grinding corn as I did, so sometimes she did it for me. That was something my husband could never do even though he was kind. It would look too bad for a man to grind corn. I found the man-woman very convenient.

I lived happily with those people and of course we never quarreled. Why should we do that? And strangely, soon after I had been married, I became dangerous again, for the first time since I had been danced. We told the medicine man and he thought, perhaps, I should be danced again and my husband, too. Who knows what danger there had been without our knowing it? So they danced us.

But this time it was different. I did not have to work hard because I had been through all that. I did not even have to sleep in the Little House. I slept in the big house next to my mother-in-law. My husband slept on the other side of the house. Every night we danced. Ah, we danced, we danced. All my life I had wanted to do that. In the daytime I could sleep. Sometimes I slept all day and waked in what we call the red evening to hear the rattle outside the house. Have you heard the rattle when our people come up in the night to dance? Ah, good!

The old people watched me until it was over, and then my husband and I ate the white clay together, and we could touch our heads and have salt in our food and go on as before.

One day my father-in-law said, "Should not our daughter-in-law be tattooed? Her face does not look right, all light, with no black on it." So my mother-in-law tattooed these four marks I have on my chin. I lay on the floor with my head in her lap and she pricked the lines with cactus thorns. Then she rubbed in greasewood soot. It hurts frightfully but if you keep still, the marks come out narrow and clear. If you wiggle they are all blurred. I did not wiggle, but I have seen girls whose chins just look as though black juice had run down them. Mine came out very pretty and, for four days, while they healed, I ate only cactus joints to make them blue.

That fall our people were going over to race with the River People and my husband said to me, "We will go." That is what he always said. I hoped I would get a man who would take me to the dances and I did. Always we went and always together.

Half the people from our village went, and the people from the Burnt Seeds and the Willows and the Narrow Place. We filled the road, going along on our horses. Two nights we camped and every night we sang. When we go to race another village, it is not just a race. We sing and dance for our rivals and we come with beautiful songs to please them. Sometimes my father made those songs, but this time it was a man named Fish Mouth. His songs were about the corn, and our men had made corn ears of cactus ribs with green yucca blades for the corn leaves and a green painted stalk. Ten boys and ten girls were going to carry them in the dance, and I was one.

We play a game with the village we are going to challenge. We send a man in on a horse, with his face painted black. He rides in to look at their dance place; then he stands up in his stirrups and calls out that we are coming. They all throw squash stems at him, the little hard stems with a circle at the bottom that cuts like a knife. So he bends close over his horse and gallops out of the village.

Then we come in. I cannot tell you all the running and the basket drumming and the old, old songs that are always sung between us before we race. My father made a speech to them and they to us. Then we dancers came in, two and two, boy and girl, holding high the white corn. The singers thumped on their baskets for us and all those River People crowded to listen. I cannot sing you the songs that Fish Mouth made, I must sing my father's. Beautiful, gay songs, my father always made.

> From the ocean far away
> Circling round our singing place
> Maidens came,
> Hither came
> To circle round our singing place.

My father had dreamed that song when he went far away to the western ocean to get salt from the dry beds there. The ocean is a magic place and only brave men dare go near it. But it gave my father beautiful songs.

> A boy had a feather belt
> The girls on either side
> Kept pulling and loosened it
> And when the dance stopped
> He had to tighten it again.

You see, that song makes you laugh. It does not say everything. They liked it, those River People. Their women came out to us with baskets of food on their heads, tortillas, squash, and succotash. They fed us all for our beautiful singing.

Then we collected the stakes that we bet on the race. Yes, I tell you, we bet everything. Men took off their deerskin shirts, women piled up their baskets. The River People made piles just like ours, shirt for shirt and basket for basket. Out beyond the village the horses were tethered two and two.

Out came the runners in white loincloths, with beautiful red designs on their should know them. Asking for Cactus Seed ran that day, and Running Short Wings. Short Wings was the best and our side won. My father et and a shawl.

Then all night we sang for the River People. We sent a man to find out their names and then our men made songs with those names in them. Beautiful, funny songs we sang to those people all night long and never a mistake in the names. Next day they paid us for our singing. Piles of wheat and corn they brought out to the dance place and then they called our names. But funny names they called, because this time was gay. When they asked us, we only told them funny names.

One of our singers was so fat we called him Seven-Yard-Shirt. So a River woman put a pile of wheat on the ground and she called out, "Seven-Yard-Shirt will get his pay here." He ran to get it and she threw squash stems at him, but he took it and ran away. Oh, we were loaded with wheat and cotton when we went riding home from the River Country. And dried beans and corn and extra horses that our young men led along!

After that, whenever we went to sing and to race and to dance, I went, too. Yes, that is how it was when I was a married woman.

## VII

We were careful when the first baby was coming. Our men were not going to war any more then, so I did not have to keep my husband home. That had always worried my mother, for if a man kills an enemy at such a time, his child will die a violent death. But probably the man will not kill an enemy, he will be killed himself, he is so weak from his wife's weakness. But my husband did not kill any rabbits so that the baby should not have a choking sickness, and he kept away from rattlesnakes so it should not have convulsions. I was kind to the people in our village who looked sick or ugly, and I never laughed at them, so that my baby should have a good body.

I did not know just when the time would be, but I knew that I felt pain when I stooped out of our little door. I said to my husband's aunt: "I think I will go to the Little House. I would not like such a dreadful thing to happen as for me to be caught inside the house in childbirth." "Well, go," she said. This was the first I had said to her or to my mother-in-law either, the whole thing being so new.

There was a gully behind our house and the Little House was on the other side of it. When I reached the near edge of that gully, I thought I had better run. I ran fast; I wanted to do the right thing. But I dropped my first baby in the middle of the gully. My aunt came and snipped the baby's navel string with her long finger nail. Then we went on to the Little House. My sisters-in-law said to me afterward, "Why didn't you tell us? We didn't know you were suffering in there. We heard you laughing." I said, "Well, it wasn't my mouth that hurt. It was my middle."

I stayed in the Little House, for that was what my father had told me to do. "When you have your first baby, don't come into the house. Stay out until the moon comes around again. Then go to the medicine man and be cleansed."

So I stayed alone there for a month, and the family brought me raw food, which I cooked. I ate no salt until the end of the baby's navel string fell off, so his navel would not be sore. Then my husband and I and the baby went to the medicine man, and he gave us all white clay to eat as he had given me when I became a maiden. But he did not give my baby a name. We were modern and I let a priest name him, Bastian.

It was nice in our house. My young brothers-in-law had married and I had their two wives to keep me company. Feather Leaves was one, and Singing Dawn. We girls did the cooking for my mother-in-law and left her to her baskets. At night when we ladled the gruel out of the pot, we all ate two and two, each married couple with one bowl, drinking by turns.

My mother-in-law managed our work. "Come," she would say, "get your carrying baskets. Let us go for food."

So we would go laughing out over the flat land to dig the roots or up in the hills to cut the cholla. I carried my baby in its cradle board on top of the carrying net. While we picked into a smaller basket, I leaned the carrying net against a tree and balanced the baby on top.

Once I was digging roots like that and I got very tired. I made a pile of earth with my digging stick, put my head on it and lay down. In front of me was a hole in the earth made by the rains, and there hung a gray spider, going up and down, up and down, on its long thread. I began to go to sleep and I said to it, "Won't you fall?"

Then the spider sang to me:

> Gray spider
> Magic making
> At the cave entrance hanging
> Do not think I shall fall.
> Twice I go up and down
> And I return again
> Therefore I am hanging, hanging here.

Our men went to hunt deer on the hills, because those summer days are when the does are big with young and taste sweet. Or else they worked in our field. There were so many men that we girls did not have to help weed the corn. But we took cactus syrup out to the field, mixed with water, that the men might drink it while they knelt on the hot earth, pulling a mesquite stick to and fro to cut off the weeds. They were going to be medicine men, all three of our husbands, and perhaps they already had visions, but they worked like other men. Ah, that was a clever household! Three medicine men and one man-woman.

We girls used to spend all day with that man-woman, Shining Evening. She went off with us to gather plants and she could carry more than any of us and dig longer. She ground corn with us, all taking turns at my mother-in-law's grinding slab.

Our husbands used to tease us girls. "How do we know these children running around the house belong to us! We are away in the mountains all the time and in the fields. It is Shining Evening who is with the women." Then they would laugh and say to the babies, "Run along! Over there is your daddy!" When they got us alone they would say, "Is he really all right?" We said, "Yes, just like a woman. We have forgotten he is a man."

When the summer was over and the pond dried up Where the Water Whirls Around, we took our babies and went moving over the hills, following the water. Over the mountains where you call it Mexico, there were more of our people who had water ditches in their fields. We worked for them and they gave us food. With many other villages we went, as if to war, because of the Apaches. We sent word all around with little sticks, ten or twelve, so that people might count them and know the day when we were going. Then we started out, the children and the bedding and a small grinding stone on a horse, and we women running beside with our carrying nets, with all the pots, and perhaps the baby on top. Far up in the hills, our husbands went running with their bows and arrows, looking for deer, and sometimes they met us with loads of meat on their backs.

At night we camped and my mother-in-law cooked a big pot of gruel. Next day I carried it among my pots so we could stop and eat it at midday. I used to be so hot and thirsty on that journey. Once, running at night, because it was too hot to travel in the day, I caught my foot in a rat's nest. Down I fell and broke all the pottery. My husband said, "Crazy one!" But Shining Evening was good to me on those trips. She was stronger than we women and when I was tired she carried my baby for me. No man could do that; it would not be right. Shining Evening was a great help.

The bean harvest of those Mexicans would be over when we arrived, and they let us go through their fields picking up the gleanings. We girls and our husbands worked, and my mother- and father-in-law went to and fro on our one horse taking the gleanings to a storage place in the mountains.

After that we worked for those Mexicans. We ground wheat and we carried wood and water. The men went up into the hills and hacked off the century plants and roasted them in pits to sell. And there they hunted, and brought down deer and hides to sell to those Mexicans. We women stayed at the foot of the hills and dug clay for pottery. Then my mother-in-law made pots, for she was clever. We young girls sat polishing them all day with little smooth stones. Oh, beautiful pots we made and earned our food! Shining Evening made pots, too, but for whiskey. She would sit there and laugh and say, "Here are my hands and here the clay. I can have what I want. Give me a bottle of whiskey."

Sometimes in the winter we went north to cut wheat for the River People and it was there that I dropped my second baby in a wheat field. And once my husband and I left the babies at home and went alone to harvest figs for the Mexicans. It was in the middle of summer but there were many people at home to work, so we got on our one horse and said, "Look! We will go to earn something for you."

We had never been before without the other Desert People, so we kept a good watch for the Apaches. It was a two-day journey and my husband did not sleep all night. We only dismounted for a little while and then I slept while he watched, awake with his arrow strung. But nothing happened until we were coming home.

We passed a flat place where there was a prickly pear growing. I said, "I'm going to eat some." So my husband lifted me off the horse. "Hurry up and pick some," he said. We had a basket hanging on the saddle. I picked the fruit and my man cleaned it and we filled that basket. Then we sat down to eat.

Look, the sun was just coming up. I was facing east and I looked up toward a hill that stood against the sun, and there I saw a man on a horse, with a long pole in his hand. "There is a man with a cactus pole," I said. But it was not a cactus pole. It was a lance. Only I had never seen lances, for our people do not use them. My husband said very low, "It's an Apache." I cried. He said, "Don't cry. They'll hear."

He got up and got on the horse. He took some arrows out of his quiver, strung one, and held the others in his hand ready to shoot. "Throw away that prickly pear and hang the basket on the saddle!" I turned out the basket and hung it on the croup. "Get up quick!" I stepped on my husband's foot and mounted.

The Apache stood there against the sun. He had feathers on his head and a blanket around his waist, and he carried his quiver over his right shoulder. If I had seen that before I should have known he was not one of our men. Ours carry the quiver at the waist. Imagine carrying it any other way! How would you use it?

That Apache hallooed, "Ai-i-i-i-i!" He was telling the other Apaches that there were Desert People in sight. Two more came out and there were three of them. They started coming toward us. We galloped fast and when we looked back they were following. I do not know when they turned back. We galloped all that day. When we came to the hidden water holes, we just stopped to drink, and when we were in the open land with the bare mountain looking down on it, where the Apaches hide, then we galloped, galloped, galloped.

We did not go alone to Mexico any more.

We came home to Where the Water Whirls Around in the Yellow month, when the greasewood bushes begin to flower in our own land. You know they flower before the rain, little yellow blossoms all over the flat land as far as you can see, so that they look like lights. When those flowers have gone, you see the white blossoms on the top of the giant cactus, sitting there like big white birds that have just come.

Then we picked the cactus fruit and we made our liquor. But this time I did not sit on the top of the house while others drank it. No! My husband's brothers did not take their wives to the singing, but my husband always took me. I was the best singer of them all. It was not for nothing that I had heard my father's songs. On the very first night of the singing, the messenger, whom we call Blackface, came galloping to all our houses: "Hail! Come tonight. Help us to bring down the moisture! Pull down the good clouds. Come and enjoy yourselves with your relatives." Then he always turned to me: "My relative, now the time has come when you should help us. Sing two nights, then you can go home and rest."

Then I took my baby and I went running with the other women down to the dance place. There was a little fire, and the eagle feathers strung up against the stars, and the liquor brewing, bubbling, where it was warm inside the council house.

In a great circle the men went round the fire, singing in the night to make the liquor brew. My husband walked at the head with his rattle. When we women came out of the dark to part the hands of the men and take our places between them, I stood beside my husband. There was where the best singers walked, boy and girl, boy and girl; those-who-stand-at-the-head.

> Within the Quijotoa Mountain
> There is a trembling
> The ocean water there within
> Is shaking.

It makes me want to cry, that song which brings the good rain.

I left my baby lying on a blanket, and the other women watched it. Between songs, when the men lit their cigarettes in the magic fire and smoked in the dark, I sat down to nurse the child. Once I fell asleep. My father-in-law was one of the medicine men standing in the center of the ring, turning his eagle feathers this way and that to catch the wind that was bringing rain, because it was dry yet, no rain had fallen. My father-in-law shook his eagle feather over me and drops of rain fell in my ear. Then I woke and sang again.

The medicine men made magic all night long, while we sang. They used to go to the string of eagles' feathers hanging outside the council house and shake them. If it was to rain soon, drops of rain would come whirling off those feathers. One man made a little pile of dirt and put a bit of eagle down on top of it. Eagle down is like the clouds; it calls them. Soon water came from the dry sky and wet that eagle down, so that the pile of earth was damp. Then he took up that eagle down and sprinkled all us dancers with it.

At the end of the second night's dancing, the medicine man told us when it would rain. We did not want it the next day, because that was when we drank our liquor. But after, when we were awake again and ready to plant our fields. And that was when it would come. We counted the days. On the night before rain should come, there was lightning in the south. On the next day, came the dust storm, bearing the rain on its back. And then the rain! But that was in the old days. Now the world is too old.

When the two nights' singing was over, our liquor that was in the council house fermented. Sometimes now it does not ferment in the right time, but then it always did. Then the Blackface came in the morning to call us to the Sit-and-drink. We sat in a circle outside the council house, and four medicine men sat in that circle at north, south, east, and west. My father-in-law was always one, and I sat beside him to help sing. Oh, I had a loud voice then.

They passed the liquor to the medicine men, and those men cleaned it, rubbing their hands around the basket. Then we drank, all of us, one after the other, from a cup gourd that the cup bearer dipped in the basket. Ours is good liquor. It does not make you fight and think unhappy thoughts. It only makes you sing. We sang, nodding our heads slowly back and forth, for that is the right way at the Sit-and-drink.

When the liquor was all gone we went to the houses. Each woman had brewed liquor for herself. She mixed it well and buried it in the earth to keep warm, saying to it, "Now I put you in the earth. Do you ferment and let us get beautifully drunk."

So we went to our relatives' houses, my husband and I together. He held my hand to keep me safe, and I had the baby on my back and one little child by the hand. The big ones we left home on the housetop as my mother had done. When we came to a house, the people held out the gourd to us. We drank it all and then we covered it with a song: that is what we call it. I had songs that I had learned from my father. After I had sung, they called me by the term of kinship, as we do, and said, "A fine song." I always had plenty to drink because I could sing.

When we wanted to rest from drinking, we went to our own house because no family may drink its own liquor. If we did that, our houses would burn; it would be taking back what you had given. So we held out the gourd to the others and listened to their songs. Then we vomited and were rested and went out again.

## VIII

My husband was a Coyote-Meeter. That is, when he had his medicine man's dreams, it was our comrade, Coyote, who came to him and sang him songs. It began when he went with the other men to the ocean to get salt, for that is where all our young men go when they want to meet some spirit. They gather the salt, and then they run along that great sandy place where the water is and where there are white birds flying overhead. It was those white birds that had sung to my father, but with my husband it was different.

Running along alone, he saw a dead coyote on the sand. He stopped. That coyote rose up and said, "Do you want to see something?" "Yes." My husband died right there and the coyote carried him away.

The other men wanted to go home and they said, "Where is he?" But the leader knew about these things. "He must have Met something. Let him alone."

Next morning my husband awoke and found himself lying by that dead coyote. He went back to the others but he never told them what he had seen.

Only after that he used to go out at night and Meet the coyotes. He would leave early in the evening and come back looking sick or drunk. The coyotes had killed him and taught him while he was dead. He did not tell us this in the house, but we all understood. The same thing was happening to his two brothers and had happened to his father before him. It was Coyote who Met them all.

After a while the people began to know that he had something. They would ask him to come and find their sicknesses for them, because people have great faith in a young medicine man. They think he has more power than an old one; he has not used it up. My husband had got himself a gourd rattle and some eagle feathers. We get our gourds down in Mexico where they grow them large and beautiful. He glued a handle on one with some mesquite gum and put some pebbles inside; nice little pebbles that you find in the wash among the ants. He got eagle feathers from an old man and tied them on a handle, four of them, tied two and two, beautifully wound about with string. He went to the houses and sat all night, rattling the gourd and singing, and they gave him clothes and food. We got rich.

Six children I had by my husband, for he was a strong man. I never had any trouble in childbirth. And I could tell what sex they would be before they were born. If the movement in my womb were strong, it would be a boy. I had five boys. I was unlucky with them, though. As soon as a new one came, the one before

*Medicine man's feather and rattle. Photograph by author.*

it died. I know a great deal about children, now that I am old, and I think it was the milk. We nurse our children till long after they can walk and talk. We must. We have no cow's milk. What would they eat? But my husband was such a strong man. The children came so fast. I was always nursing one while another was coming, and then the nursing one died.

Perhaps, though, it was only diseases that came by bad luck. That is what my husband said. He treated our children; they were among the first he sang for. One had jackrabbit sickness, which is a sort of coughing and choking that comes to a child so it cannot breathe. Another had dog sickness. I suppose a dog must have breathed on me with its hot breath before the child was born, because the baby had hot breath for days and days before it died.

I always knew when my children were to die. I am one who knows things, because, even though they took my crystals out, there was always something in me. Once, when my baby was sick, I dreamed that I was passing through a wash. A woman sat there with a child, and its hair was blowing back as though it was in the water, only the wash was dry. I said, "What are you doing here?" "We live here." I knew that meant something strange was coming.

Another time I dreamed that someone who seemed a medicine man again led me to a wash. It was full of babies and children, big and little, all crawling around over each other, like worms. "What does it mean?" I asked that man who took me. "It means all your children are going to die. You will have no children at your house."

But I saved one child, a girl. I gave her to my mother to nurse, because an old woman can nurse with us, as well as young ones. That girl grew up. She used to sit on my head when I was running along with the carrying basket, sometimes with another baby on top of it. I took her out to the hills with me when I was gathering fruit and cactus.

"Never step over a snake," I told her, "nor even the trail of a snake, for you will have the vomiting sickness. Don't step on a horned toad, it will make your foot sore. And you must learn the difference between the big ants who are the medicine men and who sting and the little kind ants that will not hurt you."

When all our family camped for days and days, to bake the cholla buds, we made a little enclosure of boughs for our children. "Stay there and do not play hard. You will be thirsty and drink up our water." So they made dolls out of leaves and played at grinding corn with sand and little flat stones. Sometimes the children brought us something to eat. In the Month of Rain, when the birds got their feathers wet in the thunder storms so they hopped along the ground and could not fly, then our children would chase them and catch them in their hands. Doves and woodpeckers they brought in to us, and we roasted them on a spit with the feathers on.

We like children, you know. We talk to them quietly and tell them what to do, but we do not scold. When our children are running about the house, in and around everything, we let them run. If they break something, then that thing is just broken. We do not say anything. Sometimes they run across the circle when we are dancing. Or when the medicine man is going about with his branch of thorns, removing sickness, they might try to grab it. No one would speak about that. We like them to be happy.

I took my little girl with me when we went to dance and sing for the River People. Every year or two we went, we three or four villages that were relatives.

Once we went to The Spring, and Begging for Yucca Fruit made the songs. Then we went to Sacaton and my father made them. The River People came to us, too, and we all went and camped at the village where they were to sing. They sang at Mesquite Root, my father's village, and he put into the singers' hands cow manure and horse manure. That meant he would give them a cow and a horse. Then we went to the Narrow Place and held a great harvest festival, and my husband was one of the singers. A good time we had, roaming over the land.

Once, when my husband and I were away working, word came that my father was sick. All the family came back to Mesquite Root, but the medicine man could not help him. We all began to cry, right then, "Haya, my father!" "Haya, my elder brother!" "Haya, my husband!" It is a sort of tune. We cried all night, but he died.

We did not bury him in a cave in the rocks as our people used to do. We had been up and down to Mexico, and had seen the priests and learned many things. We laid him down and dug a grave. We dressed him in clothes, a good shirt and trousers and sandals and a red headband around his hair. We gave him a blanket and pillow, too, for the grave. Because he was an Enemy Slayer his face was painted, black to the nose and white below. His younger brother did that, for he was an Enemy Slayer, too, and had the right.

All the men of our family dug the grave, and then carried him out and put him there. They put in his blanket and pillow, because we did not sleep on mats any more. And his leather pouch, they put in, and the sticks he had for games and his bow and arrows and his good quiver of wildcat skin. Then his brother spoke: "We put you here. Stay and don't come back to frighten us." My mother said, "Make yourself at home. Be happy. Don't come back to break up my good dreams." She was crying. Then we called him again. "Haya, my father!" "Haya, my elder brother!" "Haya, my husband!"

All the relatives called him. After that, we never said his name, José María. When we talked about him we said "my father-gone," "my elder brother-gone," "my husband-gone." To hear the name would make us feel too bad. And nobody ever said that name to us because my brothers would get angry.

We divided his horses, and my sister and I each got two. My brothers and my mother got more. My brothers took the house down and moved it. Then they put it up again in another place but still at Mesquite Root where they had always lived. There my mother lived and they with her. She said to them, "I didn't bring you up to have you go off with some woman. If you were girls, I would let you go. But since you are men, this is where you should stay. If some woman loves you and falls against you, bring her home. She can cook for me." So they married and brought their wives home. I have many grandchildren from those brothers.

I went back to Where the Water Whirls Around. We lived better there because we had more horses and my husband went often to sing for the sick. People gave him clothes for that singing, and we all had clothes then, not just something tied around our waists. And all the men had trousers instead of breech clouts. My husband and I built a house next door to his family. Shining Evening built one, too, and lived there alone. She used to cook beans and tortillas and have good food there. When my father-in-law died, my mother-in-law lived in that house with Shining Evening, and he was both a son and a daughter, only he was often away, drunk.

There were white men here and there on our land by that time, as there never had been. So our men began to learn to drink that whiskey. It was not a thing that you must drink only once a year like our cactus cider. You could drink it any time, with no singing and no speeches, and it did not bring rain. Men grew crazy when they drank that whiskey and they had visions. My husband did not drink. He had his visions. He said that a good man must get them as he and my father had, by suffering. But Shining Evening got very crazy. She would flirt and laugh with the men more than ever, throw gravel at them and slap their faces. Many names the men got from Shining Evening, for that is how our men got most of their nicknames.

She gave to her brother, Thundering Wings, the nickname of Skirt-string. Shining Evening was the first of us women to make a skirt that was sewed up and had a drawstring. Her brother pulled it out and said, "Hey! What's this!" She giggled and said in her funny high voice, "Skirt-string! Skirt-string!" So everybody called him that. Some men wanted to buy the name, it was so funny.

I was much with Shining Evening and the women in those days because my husband was away. People would send for him from far across the desert, and he would go and sing for many nights. Then on other nights he would come to me looking strange and say, "I am going to hunt rabbits." I knew it was not rabbits, but no woman questions her husband among our people. So I lay alone on my mat, thinking that, perhaps, just now my husband was with Coyote. I wondered what the Comrade would say to him, and if he would sing any songs like those I had heard from my father. Then, once, Coyote came to me, too.

I was at Mesquite Root, gathering giant cactus with my family. I always went there in the Cactus month because Mesquite Root was in the hills, near the cactus grove. Once I had picked my basket full of cactus fruit and I was resting. I looked down by my bare toe and there lay a crystal.

I have told you how medicine men find these crystals by magic, after a dream. Those shining stones have power and they can make rain. No one finds them by chance. So when I saw that, I was afraid. It was a big crystal, thick as my finger and as long as two joints of it. I took it home, but I had no use for a crystal then; my heart was cool. I gave it to my brother who was now a medicine man, and he whirled it around and tried to make rain. But he could not: the stone was not for him.

So I took it home. But I could not keep it, I, a woman, who was not meeting any spirit. I was afraid of it, and I gave it to my young brother-in-law. He is an old medicine man now, at Where the Water Whirls Around, and he has it yet.

But that night Coyote came to me. He did not speak. He looked at me a minute and then he turned away. As he went, he sang:

> A frog medicine man
> With spotted back
> Lies somewhere on the ground
> Looking for rain.
> Where, where is the rain?

Sick people came often to my husband and his brothers because they were all medicine men, and their father, too. We women, if we had wanted to, could have learned many lovely magic songs and could have looked in their medicine bags and seen the crystals and the feathers and other powerful things. Of course we did not, for those things can make you sick. We knew where the gourds were kept in the thatch of the roof and the long eagle feathers with them, but we never even looked that way. We thought we might begin to menstruate and take away their power.

But sometimes when babies were brought to my husband I could not help looking on, because I had had babies myself, and they had died. There is one thing that happens to babies that is very dangerous. They have a soft spot on the top of their heads. It is there when they are born and then it closes up. But sometimes it does not close. One who is wise will put a finger in the baby's mouth, far back and will push up. That pushes up the whole head and closes that soft spot which really comes because the head has fallen in.

My husband knew this and I have heard him tell mothers about it. But the mothers could not do the pushing. It must be a person with power.

I do not think it was crystals, for I was too old to have them grow within me any longer. Yet once, when I was at Cactus Camp, I was sick. We did not have a medicine man; my husband and his brothers were far away. I lay there, and my head spun round, and I was hot and cold. Then, out of the desert, a furry, gray coyote came trotting to me. He blew on me as the medicine man blows and I felt cool. I began to sing:

> Coyote, my comrade
> Hither ran.
> To the end of his tail
> A cloud was tied.

I felt that cool beautiful cloud, and I saw how funny Coyote looked, waving it over me and running away. I got well.

Then one day, when my daughter was twelve years old, my husband took another wife.

## IX

One day I went with my little girl to buy meat at a neighbor's house where they had just butchered. I came back and, under our arbor, there sat a girl. The relative that lived next door to us called over and said, "My elder sister, your husband's married."

Most men did not take two wives with us then, but the medicine men always did. In fact, they took four. But I had never thought my husband would do it. You see, we married so young, even before I had really become a maiden. It was as if we had been children in the same house. I had grown fond of him. We starved so much together.

The other woman spoke to me. "I see you're his wife. You had better take care of him. It's not my fault." I knew that. I knew they brought her over to our house just the way my mother brought me. Perhaps she did not know he had a wife till I came back from buying meat. I said, "I know it isn't your fault. But I am going home."

I piled my clothes in a basket, and I put in a large butcher knife. I thought if he followed, I would kill him. Then I took my little girl and went away. It was late evening. I went to the house of a relative and asked to stay the night, and early before morning-stands-up, I got up to walk to Mesquite Root, across the valley. Before I started, my husband came. He stood there and looked at us and he said to my little girl, "What will you do, go with your mother?" "Yes." He said, "Go on. I'll come to see you sometimes." He thought it was a joke.

In the afternoon I got to Mesquite Root and told my brother. He said, "All right."

Next day we were all in the field, eating watermelons, and there my husband came. My brother said, "What do you want?" "I just came after these people." My brother was angry. My husband said, "Her father came and proposed to me for her. It seemed a good thing." He meant that woman. But my brother sent him away and so he went. I did not say anything. I thought my husband would send away that woman and come back.

A few days later my uncle found out. He said, "We cannot have this woman here with no one to care for her. We must find a husband. We must show that other man that he cannot get her back." So he went to an old man and proposed for me. That old man was the one who had danced me when I became a maiden.

He had had a wife then, but now she was dead and he was living alone. He was a rich man; he had horses.

He was a distant relative of ours, one whom I called my elder brother. My father would not have allowed me to be offered to him, for we do not marry relatives. When my brother spoke to him, he said, "Very well, my younger brother. I will be there in two days."

My brother and my uncle came and told my mother and me. I cried. My mother said, "Wait. Her husband will be sorry and come for her. They have been together since they were young." But my brother would not. "Mother, you'll see. This man may be old, but he has something. He may take care of her and of you, too. That's one of my reasons." You see, my family was poor then.

I did not say anything. No woman has a right to speak against her brother, even if he is younger, as this one was. And my mother had no right either, against the men. My brother said to me, "Look here, he has something. He may be a help to you and to me." I knew that my family was poor. I said, "I'll see. If this man is good to me, I'll stay. If not, I'll give it up."

In two days the old man came, in the evening, on a horse. My brother spoke to him as if he was that old man's father: "If you don't take care of her, I'll take her back." The old man said, "All right." Then he told me, "I'll try to take good care of you, feed you and give you all you don't have. Now you go to sleep. Early in the morning I'll come and get you." He came and took me behind him on a horse and we went down the valley to Where the Rock Stands Up. My little girl stayed with my mother.

Where the Rock Stands Up was nearer to where the white people live than Where the Water Whirls Around. My husband had an adobe house there, not a brush house. He took me into it, and we lay down and rested. Then he said, "Since you have done this, my younger sister, look around and see your home." There was a little fireplace with a chimney, and inside there stood a box full of money. The old man raised horses and sold them to the white men and the Apaches. He opened that box and said, "Whatever you want, you buy." I had only the things I had on. I said, "I have no cloth to make clothes. And no sandals." I had come barefoot from Where the Water Whirls Around; we do not wear sandals except for long journeys. "In two days, get food ready and we'll go to Tucson. There are beans, flour, lard, wheat." So I ground the wheat and made tortillas.

We started on two horses for Tucson, not on one, as I had always ridden before. I had never been to Tucson. It was not like it is now, but there were stores. I bought a silk shawl, brown, with pink roses and long fringe. I was ashamed to spend so much but he said, "Buy another for every day." Then I would not have bought anything else but he bought a pair of shoes. I never had shoes before. He bought good pieces of calico and a canvas bag to put them in. He went to tie them on a horse, and he pointed to something in a window: "Don't you want that over there?" It was a sewing machine. I said, "What would I do with it?" So we left it and came home.

That old man had many horses. He traded them to the Apaches, and they paid him money, not food and clothes, as my first husband used to be paid. He could go to Tucson and buy any kind of food he wanted, lard and wheat and potatoes and

*House and ramada. Photograph by author.*

cow's meat. I got fat. I could not stoop over to put on those new shoes. My uncle came to see us when he was trading horses and he said, "What have you been feeding her?"

But I felt bad. I did not love that old man. I was not fond of him. I used to go in the washes and lie flat under the greasewood bushes and cry. Or I would lie on the floor in the house, when my husband was away, covered up with blankets. It hurt.

I never saw my first husband again. They told me that when he heard of my new marriage he cried. He said, "I didn't think she would take my child from me. I thought she would stay near and at last come back."

He did not say anything about leaving that second wife, but she left him. I had gone when the watermelons were ripe, and that very autumn, when the grass was dry, she went home. I did not know it. Where the Rock Stands Up was a day's run on foot from Where the Water Whirls Around. His brother came much later and told me, but then it was too late. In the spring, in the month of Cholla Ripening, he got sick. His brothers sent for that second wife and she came, but he did not want her. He used to scratch her arms as she sat beside him. Then he would stretch out his arms and call for me. In the month of Giant Cactus Ripening, he died.

His brother came to tell me. I cried. I used to go behind a hill, away from the house, and cry half the day. He almost took me with him. Does this happen to the whites? I kept thinking at night that the door would open and he would take me by the hand. I would cry out. My new husband said, "What is wrong? You always cry." I told him. "He comes and pulls me up." Next day, my husband said nothing. He got on a horse and rode far off there to the grave. He said, "Leave her alone. It's your own fault. If you come for her again, I'll dig you up and burn your bones." After that, the dead was quiet.

## X

I came to that old man at watermelon time. When the acorns were ripe I was pregnant, and next year, when they were baking cactus buds, I had a son. I had no trouble with my children by this man. Both sons they were and both grew up. Perhaps, it was because they did not come so fast. The man was old. There were three years between them.

Standing Rock was a nice place under the hill slope, with a big rock standing out like an eagle's beak just above us. There was a pond there for my husband's horses to drink; the yucca that we use for our baskets grew up on the hill; and there was good clay for pots. In the winter, when the horse pond dried up, we did not go to Mexico as my first husband's family did. We went to Tucson and worked for the white people.

In Tucson, we had a shack with mattresses in it. We could go to stores and buy chili and salt to eat with our food. And white flour that we did not have to grind. But I have never liked white flour. I feel sick and weak when I eat it. Now that I am old, I cry to my grandchildren, "Get me cornmeal flour. Or flour from the cactus seeds. Then I shall eat again."

I had strange dreams in Tucson. Once when we were there, my husband killed a jackrabbit and brought it to me to cook. I said, "Go get some chili for me to cook with." So he went away and then I heard someone walking round the house. I began to feel dizzy and sick in the heart. I picked up the scissors to defend myself.

*Chona gathering yucca. Photograph by author.*

But the steps went away. I stuck the scissors in the thatch. Then I cooked the rabbit and we had supper.

But at night, in my dreams, the rabbit came to me. It was a little girl. It showed me its ripped skin and said, "Why did you do this to me? Don't you know it is I that make you sick?" I felt crazy.

The next day my husband found a medicine man come in from the desert to sell acorns. That medicine man sang and fanned me. "It is dangerous," he said. "That rabbit had eaten a magic root. It was driving her mad, because she is one who has dreams. It is easy to make her wild. If I had not come to stop it, she might have killed one of you." It is true, I was looking at our pot stones, thinking of taking one up and throwing it.

But we only stayed in Tucson in the winter. In summer, we came back to Standing Rock and made cider and planted corn like other people. But I did not get used to Standing Rock as I had to Where the Water Whirls Around. I used to like to go back to Mesquite Root to visit.

Once when I was there, a sickness came. We called it the falling hair sickness, and no one could cure it because it came from the whites. It spread all over the country, as far as the River People. The medicine men went round with the thorny branch and tried to carry it out, but they could not catch it. In Mesquite Root, we buried a child every morning and another every night. I was glad I had no children but my daughter, and she was grown up then. But I got sick myself.

Very sick I was, half dead. Then, as I lay on the floor in my father's house, it seemed to me that two women came. One was a dead relative of mine and one was the Virgin Mary whom I had seen in the Catholic church in Tucson. They said to me, "You're sick, but get up. We want to show you something." They took me by either arm to a house like a church. They showed me a holy picture and a rope reaching to it. "Pull yourself up!" I started to do it. "Don't look down." But I looked down and I fell back into bed. They said, "If you had gone up, you would have been cured and would have known something. But we will take you elsewhere."

They took me to a square hole, wide as my arm to the elbow, and with just a little water in it. At each corner was a candle, but they were not candles, they were the blue stones which we think have magic power. That hole with the water in it, was all blue inside. Out of it peeped a baby's head, and I saw that the soft spot on the top of the head was moving.

That is the soft spot that makes babies sick. It is very soft when they are born and it ought to grow hard. But sometimes it does not and then the baby will not nurse. I had seen babies like that brought to my first husband, so now I looked, but I did not dare touch that baby I saw.

The women said, "Take your crystal, suck it and spit on the baby." I did it and the soft place stopped moving. Then it grew hard and it was healed. We moved around the water. At each corner we stopped, I saw the baby, and I spit on it again. So I learned how to cure.

When I got well, I began to cure babies. But no! I did not spit on them. That was a dream to give me power. I did what I had seen my husband do; pushed up inside their mouths to push up the soft spot. That is a good way; it always succeeds. You see, the women had told me to spit on a crystal but I had no crystal. I did what I knew, and because of the power of that dream, I could cure.

The man who is now our chief was brought to me, all the way from the Burnt Seeds. He had not nursed for two days; he was starving; his jaws were stiff. I rubbed his jaws with warm ashes and then pushed up the back of his head. Next day he nursed. His parents were so glad; they wanted to go home then. But I said, "Stay another night. You will shake the soft place loose again." So they stayed. That baby got well, and they gave me a big, a very big willow basket and a length of muslin. Whenever I went long after to the Burnt Seeds to drink cactus wine, his mother would say to that young man, "Will you not make a gift to your father's relative? She saved your life."

Once, after I had begun to cure like that, I found a crystal. I looked down at my feet when I was fetching water, and there it lay. But I did not know if a woman should have a crystal; I gave it to my husband. He used to carry it around in his pouch, even though he was not a medicine man. But once he went to the rain-drinking at the Burnt Seeds and someone stole it.

This husband was a singer. I have told you how he sang for the maidens' dances. Many, many songs he knew. I used to hear him singing all the time as he sat on his mattress in the evening. He was a clever man, too, a man who could think and count. He had a long stick of cactus rib, and on it he had kept the history of our Desert People. He began it when he was ten years old, long before I was born.

There was a great battle in Mexico, then, between our people and the Mexicans. Our people gathered all their women and their cattle into a big fort, on Elder Brother's mountain, and they tried to keep the Mexicans away. But they could not. They were conquered. We call that "the year the world went wrong." My husband was frightened in that year; he a little boy and hearing of all those people dead. So he got a long stick and made a mark on it, to remember. Every year, after that, he made a mark and some strange figure in blue or red to tell what had happened that year.

All our people used to come to hear that history, and he would sit on his mattress, blinking his eyes, for he was already getting blind. He would put his thumb on a mark and tell them all that had happened that year with the names of the people who ran in the races and who made the dancing songs, and what nicknames were given. All the way from one end of the stick to the other, he would go and never forget. While I lived with him, those marks stretched farther and farther down the stick. He put his marriage to me on it. When you see the stick, you will find it there.

This husband was one of the clowns who makes the people laugh at our great harvest ceremony. The clowns wear masks, you know, great white bags of deerskin, pulled down over their faces with tiny eyes painted on them and just little holes to see through. They talk in a squeaky voice because we think the clown is a magic person who comes from far in the north and talks a language we do not know. So when we went to the harvest festival and I saw the clown, I never knew it was my own husband.

He and I always went to the harvest festivals. He was good to me; he took me everywhere. I have been lucky in my husbands; I never had to stay home.

The festival was always at the Narrow Place where Elder Brother told us to have it in the beginning. We all went there with our teams, starting ten days early. We took with us cornmeal and grinding stones and plenty of dried food, so we could entertain all our relatives when they came to our camp. There we cut branches and put up little shelters for ourselves, but we did not need much for it was in the month of Pleasant Cold.

All day long our men went away to practice in the big shelter where the singing was to be. We heard their songs floating over to us, we women, and we were glad. Of course, we did not go near the shelter. Those songs are for men, they are very sacred things. You cannot ask any Indian woman about the harvest festival. That is a thing from which we keep far away.

But we were happy. We cooked all day long, on the little fires outside our shelters. Always some relative was coming to stand there and smile at us: "My elder sister!" "My younger sister!" "My father's younger sister!" "My mother's older sister!"

When one came who had had someone die since we saw her last, we all stood there and cried in the sunshine, to show her how we all felt together.

In the evening, when we were getting supper ready, the clowns would come running to all the camps squeaking in their sacred voices and holding a basket out for food, to feed the men in the Big House. Then we all gave them food, and we were afraid of them, too, because clowns have much power. Once I put tamales in the clown's basket, and there, under the white blanket that was tied around him, I saw a piece of my husband's trousers. "I'm not going to give you anything more," I said. "I know you now." The other women said I must not speak like that. They were afraid. So I kept on giving him food.

At the festival, my husband cured the sick people. Everybody who feels badly sits in a row at that feast and they call to the clown, "Cleanse me!" So he comes and blows over them and then they are well.

People used to come to my husband even when we were home again at Standing Rock. Anyone who had done wrong at the harvest feast would come to him; those who had danced or sung wrong or, maybe, fallen down when they were carrying some sacred thing. That can make you very sick, perhaps, so that you cannot walk any more.

My husband would put on his white mask, with the big bunch of turkey feathers on top. He kept that mask in a jar, far out in the hills behind our house. You must not keep such things near you. They are too strong. Perhaps you would die from their power. But he would go out all alone and get it, and come back from the north, wearing it. Then he would blow on the people. If they were very sick indeed, he had to have singers to sing the harvest songs and make the harvest feast again for that sick man. That is the way to get well.

When my oldest boy was twelve years old, my brother died, back at Mesquite Root. That was the brother who was a medicine man. He had been well known for a long time. He used to give the white clay to drink to maidens and to babies. Often I have seen him mix it up with owl feathers though no one is supposed to know that is how he does. But there are many medicine men in my family. I know.

My brother had two children and a wife, but all of them died. He could not stop it; I think it was the power of some evil medicine man. Then he himself got sick. A medicine man tried to suck out the sickness but it was too late; he was already spoiled inside. There was no one at Mesquite Root to take care of him now; my mother was very old. So I went back to stay. He lived two months and he taught me many cures. "Now you must stand in my place," he said. And he told all the people, "I am going to die but she will take care of you."

He told me how to cure sick people by rubbing up and down their legs. I can feel if there is a lump inside them and I work it out smooth. Sometimes I give them castor oil. Do you think I did not learn that from my brother? I do not know. I am old and have had many visions. He told me how to put a feather in my mouth, and after that, to spit blood. I can do that, but when I have the blood, I do not throw it away; I swallow it. This is a very mysterious thing. I tell few people that I have such power.

I got the feather in a magic way. I was sitting in the evening in our doorway, waiting for my son to come home from tending the horses. A little bird came and sat above the door and began calling. I did not understand. But at night, when I was asleep, the bird came again, and then, in my dreams, I could understand. He said, "You think I am only a little bird, but it is I who make the night go and the morning come with my singing." He sang a little tune:

> I am the kukuli bird
> You do not know
> You do not know.

Next day I found the feather he had dropped when he sat above the door and that is the feather I use.

Coyote came to me after that. I belong to the Coyote division of our people and he comes to us; never to the Buzzards. He came when I was asleep at night and said, "Look. A time will come when this world will end. People are dying now." I knew that. It seemed to me I heard all the time that someone was dead. We never used to hear that. Only once in a while, a long while, word would come that some old person was gone. But now we hear it all the time.

Coyote said, "If you want to, you can cure them. If not, they will die." I said, "I'll see."

Then he showed me how to take the blood that I could draw from a feather and rub it on a sick man's body, where his own blood did not run. That is what makes people sick. Their blood does not run. But Coyote told me, "Don't fool them. If you find you can't cure, sit back. Do nothing." Then he sang this song about himself; how he tried to cure and could not:

> Coyote, my comrade
> Spit on his fingertips
> One by one.
>
> He put his hands on the sick man
> And felt around
> "Haya, sickness!
> I can't find you!"
>
> I tried
> I could not see.
> I sat back.

So always I sit back if I cannot cure. But I could have cured if I had not given away my crystals. Yes, I could have done much.

## XI

My sons grew up. The first one we called Vincenzo but he bought the name Two Bits from another man because he liked it. We say that name in our language of course. It sounds good.

We married Two Bits when he was seventeen. Some people came to us and said, "We have a daughter. She was married to a man, but that man went away to the white school, and when he came back he did not take her." "She is older than your son," they said, "but she is industrious. She may be some help to him." We said, "It is true she is older, but we have seen her work. She may be a help."

So we told our son and he said nothing. Her mother brought us that girl, and ever since she has stayed with us and behaved herself like a woman. Some wives are like this: when their husbands are away, they run out to visit. She never does. She is always home working. Many children she and my son had, so that I have grandchildren and great-grandchildren. They live still in that flat place at Standing Rock, and when I go there, they have cactus seed for me to eat.

I went there last year before the husband of my granddaughter died. That man was sick and I could do nothing for him. I sat in their house making baskets, and a little blackbird came and drank out of the water I use to wet the fibers. I told one of my grandchildren to chase the bird away, and it went into the corner of the room. That night the bird came to me. It said, "Why did you chase me from your water? Don't you know I will need it?" I knew that man would die. So that day he did. The next night he came again, with black feathers and a cow tail. "See," he said, "how pitiful I look." I knew the devil took him.

My second son was a medicine man. Ah, that one would have been great! When he was small, he acted strange; his heart was feeling something coming. He would run out in the night, and his father would run after him and find him lying face down in the greasewood. Maybe something had come after him and taken him away.

Once, when a rattlesnake bit me, he cured me. I was picking beans among the weeds in our garden and, along with a handful of beans, I grabbed the snake. I had hold of him near the head but he turned his head back and bit my wrist. My son killed the snake. Then he chewed some greasewood leaves and put them on the little hole where it had bit me. He made a mark with a buzzard's feather all around my wrist and told the poison not to go beyond that mark. Then he split the feather and tied the two pieces into a string. He bound that string around my wrist, tight, and the poison never went beyond it. Two nights it hurt me and my hand swelled, but not beyond where my son had made the mark.

He used to bring birds home to the house and keep them; he could speak with birds. Once he kept a hawk in our house and killed jackrabbits for it. Once I saw him coming home in the evening after he had been after the horses, and there was something shining on his shoulder. It was the eyes of an owl. "What will you do with it?" I said. So he let it fly away. But I think he spoke with it after that, behind the mountain.

He had crystals growing in him, and I know he had dreams but he had not told them yet. People only tell their dreams when they begin to cure.

When he was seventeen he went to the drinking ceremony, and he met one of those wild women who run about without husbands and sleep in the arroyos. He put her on his horse and brought her home to Standing Rock. That was a bad thing. I did not like that, but we said nothing. Then she wanted money to buy things. She did not want him to stay and plant our corn with Two Bits. They went to the white man's town of Many Cottonwoods and had two children there. But that woman killed him.

She was a woman who would not wait and do things at the right time. She lay with my son in the house when she should have been at the Little House. That kills the power of a medicine man. It rots his crystals and after a while it kills him, too. So he came back to stay with my daughter and left that woman. She would not come back with him, out of the town.

I went there to my poor son and took him to a medicine man, but that one said, "His crystals are all dead and dried. They build combs like bees and those combs are empty and blue. His power is dead." So he died. "My mother," he said to me, "I will come to you like an owl. You will know me." And it is true. The other day I was passing by a giant cactus, and there sat an owl in the fork and called to me. It does not happen often. I would like to hear my son call again.

That wild woman who was his wife took another husband the next year at the drinking ceremony. The man's name was Jackrabbit Chief and he was an old man, but it was dark and she did not know it. She got on his horse with him and she said, "Where do you live?" "At the place of the Dead Dog," he said. The sun was coming up just then and she saw his face. "Oh, that's too far." She jumped off the horse and we have never seen her again.

My daughter never lived with us very much. She lived with my mother and my brother, so when it came for her to marry, it was my brother who offered her. There was a man named Crooked Lightning whose sister was married to my brother. Crooked Lightning was as old as my brother. He was a singer and a good man. He had a wife who scolded him but he did not scold her. Only one day he went away from her and came to my brother, and said he needed another wife. So my brother gave him my daughter, Crescenza. She is a big fat woman now, a good woman.

It has been a long time since my children were married. My old husband and I lived with them, and then we lived with our grandchildren. Thirty years my husband and I were together. He grew blind. He lay on his mattress all day long, and I had to pull it round the house to keep it in the shade. All the time he sang. He knew every song in the world, and he lay there singing in a low voice. Sometimes he slept in the day when it was warm and he sang in the night. We would wake up in the night and hear him singing.

Seven years ago he died. He said, "Now I'm going to rest and you shall rest, too." He meant I need not work for him any more, pulling that mattress around the house.

"But I won't come when I am dead to frighten you," he said. "Only when it's time for you to go. Then I'll come to call you. But not yet, I will not call you yet. First you'll hear some man say, 'I want to marry you.'"

The next year I did. I had great-grandchildren then, but still a man came and asked me to go to his house. But I was tired. I said, "No, I am too old. I cannot cook for you."

So I stay now with my grandchildren. Don't you think my baskets are good? I make them all day—all day long, and the young women do the cooking. While I work I hear voices: "Put a turtle there! Put a Gila monster here! Here put a zig-zag." Then I seem to see a woman holding up the finished basket and I know how it will be.

I like to work at my daughter's house, at the Burnt Seeds. She has cornmeal there and cactus seeds. I can eat when I live there, and every year I go with her to the drinking ceremony. They want me, for I can sing. But when I go to someone's house I have to stay a long time before I can walk back. It is not good to be old. Not beautiful. When you come again, I will not be here.

*Chona with her walking stick. Photograph by author.*

# PART THREE | Child Training, Women, Love, and the Present

## CHILD TRAINING

The Papago child was born not into a single family but into a group. I have made some attempt to describe this group which surrounded and supported the individual so that, without it, he did not feel completely himself. All decisions were made, all actions undertaken, with the advice and help of these relatives who were, one old man told me, "the other end of his navel cord."

This was a widespread custom in former days and the People, in their torrid country, had been able to keep to it more closely than many of their neighbors. With them, a group of old and young often lived and traveled together. They had the same kind of clothing, houses, and property; the same livelihood, customs, and religion.

The child, from the very beginning, had a place as a member of this work group. He was expected to give what help he could, even if it was only carrying a few strands of basket straw across the room. The "child's world" of some modern books, with its specially planned nursery or playroom, was impossible. Children were always in the same room with adults, sharing their food and possessions, hearing their conversation.

"Weren't they in the way?" I asked. To my mind, they were badly in the way. Barefooted toddlers were constantly falling over my feet while I was trying to write in Papago the songs of some ancient leader. I longed to ask the old man to send the children out but knew he would not. In fact, I had seen children tumbling over the dancers in a ceremony. The only comment I heard was: "They will learn."[1]

Thus an older member of a work gang would speak to a new recruit giving advice, not orders. That was the tone of Lillat's advice to his children, even of the young man who suggested that his small neighbor shut the door (p. 12).

I tried a new line: "But children must sometimes be naughty—I mean, suppose some bad little boy kept hitting his sister and taking her toys—er—gaming sticks?" I could see from the pursed lips of some mothers that that boy would never have behaved so if he had been "one of us" from babyhood. However, the oldest one

[1] Underhill, 1942, p. 81.

89

finally admitted, "Then the grandfather or some older person would tell him, 'We People do not do that.' "

"But if he kept on?"

"Then he would be told, 'Do you not wish to live with us? Will you go to the Apache?' "

That was a terrifying threat, for the Apache, terrible as they seemed to the Papago, also seemed far away. A child who went outside the village in those days would find only sand. There were no exciting bad gangs to join, nothing to steal or destroy. Ambitious rebels had to turn homeward.

I prodded again: "If a child were not really bad—just selfish, forgetful, neglected his work?"

They laughed softly: "Oh, he would be told what would happen. We are all told. In the Coyote stories. We can hear them all through the year, you know— not just in winter like the ones about the Beginning."

I did not know the Coyote stories, and I had a penchant for this beguiling animal which is the Papago's only substitute for the Devil. But Coyote is no devil. He is greedy, forgetful, tells fibs, and then tries to excuse himself just like a human. Of course he suffers for it, usually by getting killed. And a grandfather telling the story can make that horribly real, so that his hearers generally decide to mend their ways. Coyote does come to life again, Grandfather admits; but human sinners might not be so lucky. Efficient moral teaching, I decided.

"You must have had *some* rules," I prodded. "Weren't there some things a child must not ever, ever do—Coyote or no Coyote?"

They nodded. Here was something they had not mentioned. They thought I knew it because it was so important; everyone must know.

"The names of the dead must not be mentioned. Because if the dead hear they may think you are calling them. And they will come and take you because they are so lonely."

"Is that rule only for children?"

"Oh, no. It is for all of us. When the children see that we obey it, they do too. And it is the same with sacred things used in ceremonies. No one should treat them carelessly, because there lies real danger."

So the older members of the working group obeyed the same rules as the latecomers! That did away with the rebellious envy which children in some other groups feel for their elders.

Now I had the Papago commandments for child training. Shearing away those elements which were peculiarities of the People, they were reduced to a simple statement: "Draw the children into your own life. Give them from birth love, companionship, and responsibility."

The terms look almost impossible in our modern, changing life. They will be more difficult for the People as their own way of life continues to change.

## WOMEN

My first weeks among the Papago were spent almost entirely with women. This was a fortunate accident. It provided an insight into one side of tribal life not usually explored by my male colleagues.

The women were usually in groups. No matter what house Chona and I were in, these relatives—for they all seemed some kind of kin—flowed in like water into a depression. They brought ground sheets, handwork, and female children of all ages.

Of course there was no spoken greeting. They could sit in the ramada, smiling, for at least half an hour. Then a toddling child might need attention, or a baby left alone for a moment might start to cry. Any woman might pick the baby up, even nurse it if she were able. Their closeness to one another seemed to me almost that of identical twins. Perhaps that closeness was normal among ancient people whose lives often depended on mutual help.

It was not only for housework that they stayed together. Their gathering of basketry materials or clay for pots was done in groups. So was their play. All the Papagos played, both old and young. They played gambling and guessing games; they raced and jumped; but always males of any age with males, females with females.

"The men were friendly," Chona had told me. "They cleared the race track, they cheered us and bet on us."

"But they did not race with you?"

"Of course not. We were too unlike. It would be like putting quails and hawks together."

"And you were the quails, I suppose. Didn't you think the hawks had more fun?"

I had strayed into the sort of talk heard from my own female friends. It did not register with Chona. I found myself going on with the old argument: "Well, you're at home all the time with babies and cooking. The men travel and—and—"

"But we're not always home. We make our trips for basketry and greens."

So they did. I had been talking about a modern situation which had not yet confronted the Papago. Perhaps the early differentiation between men's work and women's was more sensible.

I let the companionable silence calm us all, then began again: "But the ceremonies! They are mostly at night when you would have time to go. Won't the men let you?"

In fact, I had been somewhat nettled by finding that at many ceremonies the sex separation was as complete as at games. When I arrived with the troop of women, I found that we must all sit in a certain place, good view or not. And if I had been using a male interpreter, he could not come to help.

The women were smiling as I have smiled at pestering children. I tried to defend my position: "I can see that you don't want to go on the men's hunting expeditions, but why could you not take part in ceremonies?"

They laughed. "Oh, ceremonies are something the men made up, you know. They have the dreams, they make the stories, then they perform the ceremony."

"But don't you dream?"

No, it seemed the women did not dream very much; and finally I got the explanation: "You see, we *have* power. Men have to dream to get power from the spirits and they think of everything they can—songs and speeches and marching around, hoping that the spirits will notice them and give them some power. But we *have* power." When I looked a little surprised, the answer was: "Children. Can any warrior make a child, no matter how brave and wonderful he is?"

"Warriors *do* take a little part in starting the children."

They sniffed. "A very small part. It's nothing compared to the months that a woman goes through to make a child. Don't you see that without us, there would be no men? Why should we envy men? We *made* the men."

That delightful attitude I should have been glad to take home with me. Perhaps it was the basis for the dignified composure that I saw women exhibit when in public. For Papago women, at least the older ones, are beginning to take some public positions. Very recently, one was appointed a judge above male candidates. Another is active in social reform. And San Xavier has a women's club, the first in America made up entirely of native American women. Must they go through a long battle of fighting for their place, or will the peaceful Papago attitude prevail?

## LOVE

"Tell us some Indian songs and love stories," my friends had written. (These were the days when eastern people knew very little about Indians except from Buffalo Bill, but they composed plenty of stories about lovers' leaps and bereft Indian maidens.) I had come across no such things among the Papago, so I asked Chona: "When you were a girl, did you dream about boys?" I remembered too late that "dream" is a technical term leading to a special status. I corrected myself: "I mean *think* about them? Think about being married?"

"Oh, yes," said Chona. "All of us girls thought about being married. We tried to be just as industrious and skillful as we could so that our parents would get us a good, providing husband."

"Hum! Songs, then. Were there no songs about boys and girls?"

Chona thought about that. "For me, yes. Once I made a song because I was growing into a medicine woman, but that I could not be. You know, I lost my crystals." Chona had never shown anger at this occurrence. She seemed to feel that it had happened in accordance with the laws of nature. She should have known better, and that was all.

I really wondered about the lack of love songs and love-making among the very young, for among the Sioux I had heard very different stories. However, the Papago girls up to childbearing age lived almost as in a convent. They worked and played with the thought of establishment in mind. Perhaps they did not awaken to love thoughts until later.

I had visited the Sioux. I knew about a young man playing a flute outside a girl's tipi, watching for her to come alone to the spring, and even flirting a bit. The difference? A Sioux did not have his bride chosen for him by the parents. He chose her himself and set up separate housekeeping, but this he could not do until he had attained honors. This, however, meant taking a scalp, moving against an enemy without a weapon and simply striking him, stealing horses, gaining horses as an honored gift. Such achievement took a good deal of time, and probably a man would be twenty-five years old or more before he could aspire to a bride.

I went back to Chona: "But after a woman was married, Chona, and was allowed to talk to men, did she never have—*excited* feelings?"

Chona allowed herself to grin, then looked tragic: "Of course. Some women went crazy and ran after men—but it was the 'scalps.' "

"Scalps?"

"The scalps that an Enemy Slayer brought home and hung from the roof of his house; they were in a bag or basket and he fed them and talked to them often as if they were his children. But sometimes he forgot, or the scalps were very strong and wicked ones. Then they would come down out of their basket like little men and run about the house. We children were only frightened and a little sick, but the grown women—ah, they went nearly crazy.'

"Then was the medicine man called?"

"Medicine man!" sniffed Chona. "What had he to do with it? The one with power over the scalps was the Enemy Slayer, the man who had taken the enemy that owned them. That man had gone through long purification, did I not tell you? And into his mind had come beautiful, strange thoughts."

"About the scalps?"

"Oh, no, not the scalps. About war, about the danger and dread of it. And then about the bravery of being a hero. Such things he would sing and the women would be cured."

"But the People hated war, did they not? Even the Enemy Slayer?" I was trying to picture the attitude of this peaceful people who seemed to regard passionate love as an evil similar to war. "But—even without the scalps! Could not grown women fall in love? Of course they loved their husbands," I hastened to add, "but—sometimes another man?"

"Of course," said Chona peacefully. "And at the ceremonies sometimes that was all right. Healthy and beautiful children are good for a tribe."

So the Desert People did make room for sexual enjoyment. But it was all brought into the picture of life as ordained from the Beginning.

I ventured one more supposition. "What about those Light Women of whom you told me? They were not charmed by scalps, were they?"

Chona smiled. "No, no. They were women who had passed their girlhood ceremony and should have been married, but they did not like to work. So they would paint themselves very beautifully with leaves and flowers on their bosoms and go to a ceremony where perhaps a man would see them. If he was feeling 'light-hearted,' (I *think* that was the word she intended) he might take such a woman home with him. But she soon got tired of grinding corn and fetching water, so she went away to the next ceremony."

"And what happened to such women in the end?"

"I think they married," Chona admitted. "But they were not very good at house-work, so they did not get the best men."

I gave up on love. Perhaps I had not asked the right questions.

## THE PRESENT[1]

In 1917, the United States cut out a section of the territory it had just purchased from Mexico and set up the Papago Reservation. It found there a group of people different from the warlike Sioux or the highly organized Iroquois. These Bean People (since part of their country was too hot to grow anything but beans) averred that they had always lived in the desert and practiced the same mode of life—farming during the summer rains, moving about during the waterless winters. In the course of their wanderings, they had acquired horses and a few cattle. Otherwise, their possessions were huts of brush or adobe and the food which they picked, hunted, or grew.

By the time of my visit, the Bureau of Indian Affairs had moved in. They allowed religious organizations, Catholic and Protestant, to begin teaching in some of the villages. Most important of all, they dug a few deep wells so that some families, at least, could spend a winter in the desert without wandering. In time, there were more wells—but how long would the underground water last?

The Papagos were usually at peace with the government. They accepted the suggestion, under Roosevelt's New Deal, that they should organize their three reservations under a constitution with majority voting instead of their ancient consensus of elders.

World War II had shaken the People as it had all Americans. Young Papagos entered the army in droves. They shared barracks with non-Indians, who were neither teachers nor enemies. They spoke English daily. For the first time, they really learned about the United States of which they were citizens.

They returned with a training for modern jobs, but there were almost none. So they took up the old migration pattern. For a generation or more, this pattern held, while the People changed from farmers to wage or salaried workers and their second language changed from Spanish to English.

Families that had worked in modern cities came back to build houses equipped with kitchens and bedrooms. Government money improved the roads and began erosion control. The U.S. Public Health Service put up a new hospital at Sells with extensions in some villages. There was little that could be done on the main desert. When President Johnson proclaimed his project of The Great Society, the reservation seemed to be inhabited mainly by the old, the blind, and the children, people chiefly on pensions.

The Great Society released a flood of new plans and millions of dollars for their implementation. The earthen-floored adobe houses disappeared. New ones were of adobe with wood trimmings, cement blocks, and sometimes wood. The Office

[1] Much information for this chapter has come from Dobyns, 1972; and Tatom, 1975.

*Ruth Underhill in her study.*
(Frank Lee Earley, Arapahoe Community College, Littleton, Colorado.)

of Economic Opportunity employed Papagos to build these, then to rent or buy them at low cost. One group of portable homes was cared for by the government, after construction, and offered free to the very poor.

Many Papagos had been away to study, and they clamored for more schooling on the reservation. In time, there were several government elementary schools and preschool programs. In 1971, the big high school was built at Sells. Most church schools have been given up at the present time. (San Xavier still maintains a Catholic school).[2]

The Sells school, with its huge grounds, is operated not by the government, but by the Arizona (Sells school district) school board. That means that the voters of the state have a voice in its affairs. Papagos are voters and much regarded at election time. Therefore, they need not feel that unusable foreign learning is being thrust upon them. In fact, they have a dictionary in their own language prepared by experienced linguists and illustrated with pictures which should make English translation interesting even for the lower grades.

[2] Some information on schools was kindly provided by **Dr. Donald Bahr, Arizona State University Department of Anthropology, Tempe, Arizona** (personal communication, June 1978).

Some ceremonies are still held in the old language, modernized and changed. The words are being written down by "Anglos" with Papago oversight. For communication among themselves, the People prefer the tape recorder, which does away with writing. With the furor now about Indian languages dying out, this has proven to be a very useful tool. If the People can talk to each other without the use of English or writing, then we need not fear the loss of their ancient language. A new field has been opened up for future linguistic study.

There is no Papago college. However, scholarships are offered by the government and various organizations and individuals. A Papago boy or girl, eager for training in some profession, can get it as easily as any other student in the United States. Many have done so. A past Council head, Thomas Segundo, studied at Arizona and Chicago universities and became an executive for the Illinois Highway Department.

For less skilled labor, there is work at the copper mine at Ajo, west of the reservation; and at the waterworks at Gila Bend, to the north.

The desert has scarcely changed. Unless some modern miracle can make it livable, its people must still move back and forth. Now they travel farther and stay longer. But they come back. The Desert People—the Bean People—are not dying out.

# Questions for Reflection

## Catherine J. Lavender, PhD
*Director, American Studies Program*
*Associate Professor, Department of History*
*The College of Staten Island/CUNY*

1. Whose story is this? Is this the story of an individual woman named Chona? Of the women of a specific Native American tribe? Of a white, eastern, urban, middle-class woman anthropologist? Of women in general?

2. What is the story? Is there a moral to this story? Does the moral change over time and in the eyes of the author and audience?

3. What concerns distinguish the 1933 introduction (by Ruth Benedict) from the 1978 introduction (by Ruth Underhill)? What does Benedict mean by the statements that "the daily task of the ethnologist is with the alien ways of acting, the alien ways of thinking, that are the traditional heritage of different peoples," and "the reader who is interested in the things men live by under their codes of right and wrong, other hopes and terrors, will find [Chona's] a real story ... of a human life among a primitive people"? Compare Benedict's 1933 statement that the ethnologist "need not fear a journalistic distortion" to Underhill's 1978 assertion that "this whole introduction, meant to show [Chona's] environment, is a memory picture of my own—true in essence." What is the difference?

4. How is this story narrated? Is there one story here or two? What is the relationship of the pieces of this story to each other? To the whole?

5. What is the significance of the land in this story for Chona and Underhill? What strategies does Underhill utilize to create its presence?

6. What is Chona getting from this relationship of informant to anthropologist? and Underhill? Is there evidence of any way in which Chona is using Underhill for her own purposes?

7. What evidence have we in the text of Underhill's reworking of Chona's story?

8. What was Chona's sense of time? Was it the same as Underhill's? What role did her sense of time play in crafting the narrative?

9. What was the Papago view of people different from them? What was Underhill's view of the Papago?

10. What evidence have we in the text about native-white interaction, and of Chona's relation to the capitalist market, in particular? What does Underhill do with this information?

11. What do we learn about female sex roles among the Papago?

12. Is there any evidence in the text of a woman's culture, a gender-specific set of values and rituals, among the Papago? How does Underhill understand this culture?

13. Is there a woman's culture which is shared by both Underhill and Chona? Does Chona believe so? Does Underhill?

14. What do we learn about marriage among the Papago? How were marriages contracted and dissolved? Were marriages monogamous or polygamous? What were the expectations for the relationship of marriage?

15. What do we learn about childbearing and rearing?

16. What do you make of Shining Evening, the brother of Chona's husband? Is she a homosexual? a transvestite? a hermaphrodite? a morphological male who takes on the female gender? Is she seen as abnormal according to her community and family? What was Chona's relationship with Shining Evening?

17. Define the terms "sex," "sexuality," and "gender." How many sexes, sexualities, and genders are there? Do sexual identity and gender identity necessarily go together? Do sexual identity and sexual behavior go together—that is, if one engages in homosexual or heterosexual behaviors, does that make one homosexual or heterosexual? What did Chona think about this? What did Underhill think?

18. Was Shining Evening a unique individual or were there others like her? If she was a man-woman, a morphological male who takes on the gender of a woman, are there examples in the text of a woman-man, or morphological females who take on the gender of a man?

19. How did Chona define true womanhood? Is Chona a feminine woman, a traditional woman, by the terms of her culture as you understand it?

20. What work did women do among the Papago? Did Chona follow these female sex roles? What did Underhill think of Chona?

21. What did her family and community make of Chona's dreams and powers? How did Chona think of them? Was the significance of her dreams and powers a life-long concern?

22. What evidence do we have about Papago gender relations? Is the Papago tribe patriarchal or matriarchal? What evidence do you have for it being patriarchal or matriarchal?

23. Underhill talks of Chona's independence and her rebellions and seems to hold her up as a kind of proto-feminist. Was Chona a feminist?

SELECTED BIBLIOGRAPHY

The following bibliography is by no means an exhaustive one but meant to acquaint interested students with some of the available literature on the Papago:

*Books and articles by the author*

Castetter, Edward F., and Ruth M. Underhill, 1935. *The Ethnobiology of the Papago Indians.* University of New Mexico Bulletin: Biological Series 4:3 (Ethnobiological Studies in the American Southwest, II).
Underhill, Ruth M., 1938a. *A Papago Calendar Record.* University of New Mexico Bulletin: Anthropological Series 2:5.
————, 1938b. *Singing for Power: The Song Magic of the Papago Indians of Southern Arizona.* Berkeley: University of California Press.
————, 1939. *Social Organization of the Papago Indians.* Columbia University Contributions to Anthropology, Vol. 30. New York: Columbia University Press.
————, 1940. *The Papago Indians of Arizona and Their Relatives, the Pima.* Education Division, U.S. Office of Indian Affairs, Sherman Pamphlets No. 3.
————, 1942. "Child Training in an Indian Tribe," in *Marriage and Family Living*, Vol. 4, No. 4, pp. 80–81. (Reprinted, 1944, in *Education for Action.*)
————, 1946. *Papago Indian Religion.* Columbia University Contributions to Anthropology, No. 33. New York: Columbia University Press.
————, 1951. *People of the Crimson Evening.* Education Division, U.S. Office of Indian Affairs, Indian Life and Customs Pamphlet No. 7.
————, 1965. "The Papago Family," in *Comparative Family Systems*, edited by M. F. Nimkoff. Boston: Houghton Mifflin Company, pp. 147–162.
————, 1966. "Papago Rain Festival," in *Quarterly of the Southwestern Association on Indian Affairs, Inc.*, Vol. 3, No. 3, Summer 1966, pp. 3–5.
————, 1974. "Acculturation at the Papago Village of Santa Rosa," in *Papago Indians I: American Indian Ethnohistory, Indians of the Southwest*, compiled and edited by David Agee Horr. New York and London: Garland Publishing Inc., pp. 309–348.

*Papago Arts and Crafts, Music*

Densmore, Frances, 1929. "Papago Music," *Bureau of American Ethnology Bulletin 90*, Smithsonian Institution. Washington: U.S. Government Printing Office. (Reprinted, 1972, New York: Da Capo Press.)

99

Fontana, Bernard L., et al., 1962. *Papago Indian Pottery* (The American Ethnological Society). Seattle: University of Washington Press.

Kissell, Mary Lois, 1916. "Basketry of the Papago and Pima," *Anthropological Papers of the American Museum of Natural History*, Vol. XVII, Pt. iv. New York: The Trustees of the American Museum of Natural History.

*Papago Economy*

Castetter, Edward, and Willis H. Bell, 1942. *Pima and Papago Indian Agriculture.* Albuquerque: The University of New Mexico Press.

*Papago Linguistics*

Dolores, Juan, 1913. "Papago Verb Stems," *University of California Publications in American Archaeology and Ethnology*, Vol. 10, No. 5, pp. 241–263. Berkeley: University of California Press.

Mathiot, Madeleine, 1968. *An Approach to the Cognitive Study of Language* (Indiana University Research Center in Anthropology, Folklore, and Linguistics, Pub. No. 45). Bloomington: Indiana University Press.

Saxton, Dean, and Lucille Saxton, 1969. *Dictionary: Papago & Pima to English, O'odham—Mil-gahn; English to Papago & Pima, Mil-gahn—O'odham.* Tucson: The University of Arizona Press.

*Religion and Folklore*

Bahr, Donald M., 1975. *Pima and Papago Ritual Oratory: A Study of Three Texts.* San Francisco: The Indian Historian Press.

Bahr, Donald M., Juan Gregorio, David I. Lopez, and Albert Alvarez, 1974. *Piman Shamanism and Staying Sickness (Ká:cim Múmkidag).* Tucson: The University of Arizona Press.

Davis, Edward H., 1920. *The Papago Ceremony of Víkita.* New York: Museum of the American Indian, Heye Foundation.

Saxton, Dean, and Lucille Saxton, 1973. *O'othham Hoho'ok A'agitha: Legends and Lore of the Papago and Pima Indians.* Tucson: The University of Arizona Press.

*Modern*

Dobyns, Henry F., 1972. *The Papago People.* Phoenix: Indian Tribal Series.

Tatom, William M., editor, 1975. *The Papago Indian Reservation and the Papago People* (A Publication of The Papago Tribe of Arizona, The Bureau of Indian Affairs Papago Agency, and The U.S. Public Health Service).

Waddell, Jack O., 1969. *Papago Indians at Work* (Anthropological Papers of The University of Arizona Number 12). Tucson: The University of Arizona Press.

*Also available from Waveland Press . . .*